WHITE GHETTO

WHITE GHETTO

HOW
MIDDLE CLASS AMERICA
REFLECTS
INNER CITY
DECAY

Star Parker

THOMAS NELSON
Since 1798

NASHVILLE   DALLAS   MEXICO CITY   RIO DE JANEIRO   BEIJING

Published in Nashville, Tennessee, by Thomas Nelson. Thomas Nelson is a registered trademark of Thomas Nelson, Inc.

Scripture taken from the New King James Version. © 1979, 1980, 1982 by Thomas Nelson, Inc. Used by permission. All rights reserved.

Thomas Nelson, Inc., books may be purchased in bulk for educational, business, fundraising, or sales promotional use. For information, please e-mail SpecialMarkets@ThomasNelson.com.

Library of Congress Cataloging-in-Publication Data on file with the
Library of Congress

ISBN 978-1-59555-027-9 (hc)
ISBN 978-1-59555-339-3 (tp)

Printed in the United States of America

09 10 11 12 13 LSI 5 4 3 2 1

In loving memory of my precious
Rachel Sarah

Table of Contents

CONTENTS

CONTENTS

CONTENTS

Introduction

For the past several decades, Middle America has found an easy scapegoat for the problems that face American society: the inner-city neighborhoods. Faced with the increase in crime rates, illegitimate pregnancies, and sexually transmitted diseases, the response of many middle-class Americans has been to point the finger at low-income and minority communities in large urban areas such as Oakland, Chicago, and Atlanta.

It is true that these problems are especially prevalent in these communities, especially those where single-mother black families reside. But what if the disproportionately higher rates of crime, illegitimacy, infant mortality, AIDS, abortion, drug abuse, and illiteracy in these poverty-stricken, inner-city neighborhoods are simply a magnified reflection of a malaise that affects every neighborhood throughout the United States? What if the inner city is actually a mirror for the rest of our nation?

Some citizens may balk at the idea that their town is anything like downtown Los Angeles. But lust and addiction are not confined to dark and desolate alleys. If they were, the rural South and Midwest would not be afflicted by methamphetamine addicts, and wealthy suburbs would not abound with promiscuity and divorce. (It was not inner-city blacks who secured the fame of shows like *Sex in the City*.)

What if the ghetto we often imagine belonging exclusively to Harlem and Watts actually has satellite campuses in Des Moines, Tulsa, Springfield, and Anchorage? Black ghetto or white, it doesn't matter—the mindset behind both is that of an equal-opportunity "employer," one who is very quickly eroding our fundamental beliefs as one nation under God. The wide-ranging apathy of our nation was obvious when Michael Newdow's continual attacks on the Pledge of Allegiance barely registered a blip on America's social radar screen.

Middle America is skilled at condemning faceless gang members whose arbitrary bullets cut short random lives. But we are blind to our own corruption. We criticize the welfare mother for not paying her own way while racking up thousands in debt on our Visa. Rather than addressing teenage sex through abstinence programs, we allow the public education system to cart our children off to abortion mills and alternative lifestyle seminars. We demand the government be held responsible for the effects of natural disasters instead of turning to God and ourselves. Our buttoned-down shirts, eco-friendly cars, and café lattes disguise morals no better than those of the drug dealers in the Bronx.

But this book is not an indictment of the excesses, failures, and sins of middle-class suburbia any more than it is an exoneration of black neighborhoods. Rather, it questions why so many obvious areas of moral breakdown exist throughout the country.

Whether you live in Compton or Kennebunkport, a radicalized progressive liberalism has pervaded Middle America and usurped the authority of our founding fathers, promising to create a newer, more tolerant America, free of the hang-ups of Judeo Christian beliefs and values. Have the proponents of this new liberalism delivered the goods of a society free of crime, racism, and poverty? Of course not. A cursory look around even our quiet bedroom communities reveals that quite the opposite has occurred.

White Ghetto calls Americans to remember the bar of religious ideals and vision that the founders of our nation set for us. It seeks to find if the legal and political battles going on in our country stem from a sincere effort to imitate the spirit of our nation's moral foundation or if they uncover a quest to dramatically change society's values and manipulate jurisprudence so that pleasure, greed, and envy can have free reign.

Middle America must ask itself some tough questions: Do the sexual madness, values disorientation, and social turmoil in our inner cities reflect the moral and cultural state of America as a whole? Does the popular system of welfare truly benefit the citizens it serves? Do ethics without a biblical basis condemn man to his animal nature? And finally, can compassionate conservatism exist without first being grounded in the most fundamental tenets of Judeo-Christian morality?

White Ghetto investigates the cultural war being waged, not on the steps of Capitol Hill, but in every kitchen, bedroom, and living room of modern Middle America. It exposes the false security behind the average American household and shows that damage from an unending assault of godless ideas has reached farther (and closer) than we ever imagined.

Welcome to an unabashed tour through America's *White Ghetto*.

SEX
IN THE
GHETTO

Of all the transformations in the moral climate of our country, perhaps the most obvious value-shift has been in the sexual arena. Gone are the days when mommies and daddies lived in the same house, TV bylaws required twin beds for the Ricardos, and few children had heard (or spoken) the *F*-word. Today's American child grows up in a taboo-free society where sex sells everything from hamburgers to shampoo. As sexual pandemonium pulsates through our nation, it wreaks havoc not only in our inner cities, but on the eroding values of Middle America as well.

AS GOES THE FAMILY . . .

To understand our nation's problems with sex, we must first look at problems with sex's divinely-planned tangible result: the family.

In 1965 Daniel Patrick Moynihan tried to point out some "family problems" in his report called *The Negro Family: The Case for National Action*. The report pointed to the breakdown of the black family and the matriarchal single-mother household as the reason for the dramatic increase in crime, illegitimate births, and sexually transmitted diseases; it also discussed the phenomenon of the transient black father. Although hailed as "prophetic" by later social commentaries like Kay Hymowitz's 2005 article, "The Black Family: 40 Years of Lies," in its day, Moynihan's report was disregarded by government leaders and maligned by social leaders as racist and sexist.

We now know that leaders were foolish to ignore Moynihan's

warning. Back then one in four black children were born out of wedlock; today, it's three in four. And yet, the same driving force of progressive liberalism that denied an honest look at the structure of the black family in the 1960s has cunningly molded thought in the predominantly white and/or middle-class neighborhoods through the decades as well. In the history of this country, there has never been a lower probability that a child of any race will grow up in a family with both parents present. America's future promises to have a majority of working adults who have no memory or concept of a traditional home.

Indeed, forty years after America's leaders ignored Moynihan's alarm, the effects of the breakdown of the family were painfully obvious when Hurricane Katrina hit New Orleans in September of 2005: The majority of the impacted citizens were poor and black. Talking heads across the nation blamed President Bush for the ensuing chaos, closing their minds to other possible contributing factors. One glaring statistic they ignored was that approximately 60 percent of all births in New Orleans were out-of-wedlock. Could this be one reason why thousands upon thousands of New Orleans' citizens were unable to leave the city prior to and after the hurricane? Many of these "families" had no father or husband to lead them out, provide them with the necessary shelter and food, or protect them from the appalling conditions that followed.

Unfortunately, out-of-wedlock pregnancies and abortions are prevalent among minorities and those living near or at the poverty level in the large, urban areas of our nation. The National Center for Health Statistics (NCHS) reports that in 2002, the rate of births for unmarried Hispanic women was 87.9 per 1000 births, with African American women rating second highest at 66.2 per 1000. The abortion rate for both of these minority groups was equally staggering. Figures from the NCHS (2001) study show that for every 1,000 black women, 29 abortions are performed, and for every 1,000 Hispanic women, 22 abortions are performed.

When the out-of-wedlock birth rate among black women reaches 75 percent, it's easy for many Americans to blame black neighborhoods for the ills facing much of the inner city, and consequently, of society. But it's important to remember that black social problems are symptomatic of a national problem. Irresponsible sexual behavior has no racial boundaries. For example, the rate of illegitimate births among whites today exceeds the rate among blacks forty years ago. America is approaching the day when one out of every three babies will be born out-of-wedlock.

Do Americans find such blatant immorality offensive? Hardly. Today almost 60 percent of Americans believe that it is morally acceptable for an unmarried man and unmarried woman to have sexual relations. Fifty-four percent see no problem with producing a child outside of marriage, compared to only 43 percent who disapprove.

I don't know about you, but I can remember the days when a single girl who got pregnant went off to live with her aunt in the boondocks and wasn't heard from again for a long time. I am certainly not advocating that parents disown their young, unmarried, pregnant daughters. But I do want to know how we ever came to the place of such overt, public, and socially accepted sexual sin. Why have so many Americans abandoned the moral codes passed down by our forefathers?

Many of you may be thinking, "My forefathers—my father

for that matter—didn't pass anything down to me!" Indeed it is true that some biological fathers are anything but loving familial and spiritual ones. By abandoning their important role in the family, too many American fathers have ensured that with each passing decade, we are becoming more and more a nation of moral moderates. (For anyone politically minded, America's downslide in morals is no respecter of parties: in 2005, 63 percent of Democrats and 51 percent of Republicans said that sex outside of marriage was acceptable.)

MIDDLE AMERICA'S FATHER: ABSENT WITHOUT LEAVING

The devastating effects of the absent urban black father have been much discussed. But what role have Middle America's fathers played in the values war raging in our country? Are they steering their families away from our culture's immoral landmines? If you haven't noticed, most (with the exception of some outspoken evangelical leaders and talk-show hosts) are suspiciously quiet, too wrapped up in stocks and bonds or the sports page to engage in any ethical squall. Or maybe they're just watching TV. . . .

Television networks offer a variety of mind-numbing entertainment for the dedicated couch potato. In the early 2000s, America's number one sitcom was *Everybody Loves Raymond*, a show featuring an overly passive and sophomoric husband, Ray Barone, who cares almost as much about his role as a father as he does about his golf game. Raymond's persistent nemesis and wife, Debra, has to kowtow her husband into taking out the garbage. She is the main adult in the family, the one who handles the difficult issues and dysfunctional in-laws. And this show, glorifying male mediocrity, is the highest rated television comedy?!

I know that the show is supposed to be a comedy. I know entertainment producers would say to "lighten up" and not take things too seriously. But the best of all comedy is based on truth. If Raymond Barone (I know nothing of the personal life of Ray Romano) is the epitome of the American male, then our offspring have much to worry about. What would Raymond do in times of national crises such as 9/11? What would Raymond do to defend his wife and children if a thief broke into the house? What would Raymond do if his wife wanted an abortion or if one of his kids got hooked on methamphetamines? Would good old, "man's man" Raymond have a clue? Of course not! His is a world of superficiality and donuts. That is why we laugh at the caricature of Raymond—he is today's lovable male prototype. He represents a very real and very large segment of American society, the ultimate expression of the Moderate Middle.

I will say one thing for Raymond, though, at least his show's content is rated PG. That's more than I can say for the junk targeted at our nation's teenagers.

FROM *OZZIE & HARRIET* TO OZZY & SHARON

We have found the perfect babysitter in Mr. TV: always available, always entertaining—and many children's primary instructor from toddler-hood on.

Television doesn't discriminate—99 percent of our homes

have at least one set. America's children watch an average of three-and-a-half hours of TV each day, or twenty-four hours per week. By the time Johnny graduates from high school, he will have spent 18,000 hours in front of a TV. And what will his malleable little mind have ingested? One hundred thousand acts of violence, including 8,000 murders, by the sixth grade. As for sexual content, let's just say that youthful innocence has been thrown out with yesterday's remote control.

According to a 2005 study by the Kaiser Family Foundation, 70 percent of today's television shows include some sexual content, with an average of 5 sex scenes per hour. Viewers craving even more titillation can tune into the top teen shows, averaging 6.7 sex scenes an hour. If our "liberalized" society continues its pattern, these nasty numbers will only rise, considering the number of sex scenes has doubled since Kaiser's first study in 1998. Take heart, though. Studio executives have made sure to combat the sex featured in 70 percent of their shows with a word about "safe sex" in 14 percent of the lineup.

But those statistics are meaningless anyway, right? Just because kids *see* sex doesn't mean they'll *have* sex. In 2004 a group of behavioral scientists funded by the National Institute of Child Health and Human Development asked that very question and published their results in the Rand report.

What did they find? After following over 1700 adolescents (ages twelve to seventeen) for a year, their report confirmed the obvious. Namely, that:

- Watching TV shows with sexual content apparently hastens the initiation of teen sexual activity.

- Watching the highest levels of sexual content effectively doubles the next-year likelihood of initiating intercourse and greatly increases the probability of advancing in other areas of sexual activity.

- Sexual talk on TV has the same effect on teens as depictions of sex.

- Sexual content on TV is far more likely to promote sexual activity among US adolescents than it is to discourage it.

Although the study agreed that other factors also encourage early sexual activity—being older, having older friends, getting lower grades, and engaging in rule-breaking activities like skipping class—it ultimately found that youths who watch the most sexual content on television "act older." In other words, a twelve-year-old who watches a lot of sex behaves more like a fourteen- or fifteen-year old who watches a little.

Unplanned pregnancies and STDs are more common among those who begin sexual activity earlier. Currently, one out of every four sexually active teens in the United States is diagnosed with a sexually transmitted disease, an estimated four million. The U.S. rate of teen pregnancy, 750,000 per year, is among the highest of all industrialized countries. Researchers say that even a moderate decline in the sexual content of adolescent shows could substantially lower sexual behavior in the teenage population. Faced with these facts, you might think that television producers would feel a responsibility to severely limit the amount of sex on teen shows. However, when confronted, television executives respond with the token liberal response to any question about vulgarity in the media: "If you don't like it, turn it off."

Though I hate to agree with filth mongers, they have a point. Parents must take control—of their remotes and their teens. The Rand study confirmed this by finding that teens who were most likely to avoid or delay sex were those whose parents monitored their activities and clearly disapproved of them having sexual relations. Middle America's parents must assume their role as guardians of their children.

MUSIC TODAY: NO SHOES, NO SHIRT, NO MORALS

A little contraption called the iPod gives teens access to songs in a way none of us growing up with 8-tracks and LPs ever dreamed. Unfortunately, it can also transport a constant stream of audio pollution into young ears and minds.

Listen to five minutes of a station playing hip-hop and rap for a sample of today's "taste" in music. The rap that permeates black communities supposedly reflects the lifestyles of inner-city youths in particular and the plight of all blacks in general. In reality these songs don't just reflect the moral poverty in the projects; they encourage it. Lyrics from Snoop Doggy Dogg's innocently titled "Puppy Love" describe a man celebrating his sexual conquests and explaining why he is enthralled that he lost his virginity at such a young age. In the final verse, Snoop shows his appreciation to a certain girl that "converted" him to a life of "pimpin'":

Sometimes I sit and think of how I used to be
Before I got converted to a D-O-double G
I'd like to thank that girl
From way back in the days
Cause if it weren't for you I wouldn't pimp this way

With all the millions he's made from selling his soul, Snoop Dogg can afford to celebrate pimpin' and a life of depravity. Those living in poverty-stricken urban areas who suffer immorality's effects have no way of escape. Indeed, millions of African Americans don't applaud the gangster lifestyle; a majority (63 percent) of the black community claim to be "born again." Even so, most of these evangelical, full-gospel, goin'-all-the-way-with-Jesus mothers (and fathers, if they are in the home) allow their children to purchase Snoop Dogg's and other notorious rappers' music.

This isn't just a black issue. In a prime example of integration gone awry, white adolescents have bought tens of millions of dollars worth of rap music over the last decade. Critics praise white rappers Eminem and Kid Rock for the same musical "genius" as Dr. Dre and Tupac Shakur, and their albums make millions in the heartland of America, the Red States. For an example of these rappers' so-called brilliance, read some lyrics from Kid Rock's "You Never Met a Motherf***er Quite Like Me":

Yep
I've been on the cover of the Rolling Stone
I met the president when I was half stoned

I been so high I've gotten confused
I been beat down, broke and used
Motherf***er

(Language like that used to earn young men a bar of soap; today it gets them Grammy awards.)

Musical trash isn't confined to rap; pop and boy-band artists offer up some equally shameless lyrics. For example, Christina Aguilera explains what she expects when she goes to a party:

Ah, dirty (dirrty)
Filthy (filthy)
Nasty (Christina), you nasty (yeah)
Too dirrty to clean my act up (haha)
If you ain't dirrty
You ain't here to party (woo!) . . .
DJ spinning (show your hands)
Let's get dirrty (that's my jam)
I need that, uh, to get me off
Sweating till my clothes come off

I shudder to think of all the pre-teen girls who stare at Christina's poster every night when they go to sleep. And yet the same parents who allow their children to purchase this young woman's music complain about the way they dress. After listening to most of today's songs, it's a wonder that teens want to wear anything at all!

No community, wealth, or religious affiliation can immunize young people to the effects of the pervasive in-your-face sexual content of today's popular music. Brittany Spears and Jessica Simpson, women who today don't know the difference between a dishtowel and a bathing suit, were supposedly raised as Christians. Spears attended a private Christian school in her hometown in Louisiana and encouraged abstinence during the early part of her career. Judging from the lyrics of one of her more recent songs, "Boys," the singer has changed her tune:

> *What would it take for you to just leave with me?*
> *Not tryin' to sound conceited but*
> *You and me were meant to be (yeah)*
> *You're a sexy guy, I'm a nice girl*
> *Let's turn this dance floor into our own little nasty world!*

Adding fuel to the fire of sexuality in music are the videos served up twenty-four hours a day on MTV and VH-1. To promote last year's movie flop *The Dukes of Hazzard* in which she played Daisy Duke, Jessica Simpson starred in her own music video rendition of "These Boots Were Made for Walkin'." In it, Jessica shows less of what Jesus would do and more of what Jessica would do with a pink bikini and a bucket of soap. Jessica's shorts were too tight to fit even a small Gideon's New Testament Bible in her back pocket. (Maybe that was her way of spreading the Gospel—attract them with some eye candy and then, when they're not expecting it, lead them in the Sinner's Prayer.)

The total number of Britney Spears albums sold has topped fifty-five million in just five short years. If those sales occurred only in the United States, that would mean that approximately 19 percent of Americans purchased at least one Britney Spears album. A government Web site estimates that in 2003, the number of (U.S.) children ages 0–17 was seventy-three million, approximately 25 percent of the population. From that information, it can be assumed that an overwhelming majority of American pre-teens and teenagers own Spears's music and have watched images of her writhing with boa constrictors or kissing Madonna. What mindset are we developing in our children, the future generation of adult Americans, by allowing them to purchase music and view images that would have been considered X-rated prior to the 1980s?

But that's just it: what we as Americans allow or don't allow makes the difference in the moral climate of today and tomorrow. While it is easy to blame the Snoop Doggs and the Jessica Simpsons of the world, their popularity hinges on the free market—on our decision to purchase or not purchase their material.

Likewise with television sitcoms and dramas; they survive or die based on ratings. If we don't watch a show, it doesn't remain on the air. Television sponsors are all too aware of consumers' power and can thus be hypersensitive about content. So what if their concern is more about money than ethics? If we put our money where our mouth is, they will listen. Middle America must stand up and say "no" to our children when they want to purchase music, movies, or clothing that conflicts with our moral worldview. We have to be brave enough to walk out (or better yet, never buy a ticket) of the movies that offer images and ideas contrary to our beliefs. A friend of mine walked out on *Titanic* simply because it promoted the notion that it is all right to have an affair with someone else if your fiancé is a real jerk. Another friend left *Midnight in the Garden of Good and Evil* because of its indulgence in the macabre and witchcraft along with its acceptance and promotion of homosexuality and cross-dressing. And yet, while thousands of middle-class parents across America enjoyed a free Saturday night, their teenage sons and daughters made the vulgar *American Pie* a blockbuster? If we are the country that voted for our current president because of his moral platform, we better act like it.

"FIRST BASE" HAS MOVED

Remember the joy you felt when you first held hands? The thrill of your first kiss? Sadly, today's adolescents will remember other firsts. America's *Sex in the City* society has not been lost on our teenagers; our children have gone way beyond watching and listening about sex. Today, activities formerly associated with porn stars and prostitutes are now connected to presidents and preteens.

A recent study on the sexual behavior of teenagers by the Centers for Disease Control and Prevention revealed that more than half of American teenagers from fifteen to nineteen years old have participated in oral sex.

The AIDS crisis of the 80s apparently motivated people to want to "play it safer" in their sexual habits, leading to an increase in oral sex. Add to that a virtual decree by President Bill Clinton that oral sex isn't really sex, and teens' raging hormones were set free—after all, it's safe and you can still be considered a virgin! (Outdated standards at least have an honorary status).

Sarah Brown, director of the National Campaign to Prevent Teen Pregnancy, told *USA Today* that adults consider oral sex to be "extremely intimate, and to some of these young people, apparently it isn't as much. . . . What we're learning here is that adolescents are redefining what is to be intimate." Now isn't that sweet? No need to fret over the corruption of our teens, let's praise their ingenuity instead!

Adolescent oral sex commonly occurs outside of the confines of a steady, monogamous relationship (ever heard of "hooking up?"). Parties are a point of rendezvous, at times allowing for multiple partner interactions. Giving new meaning to the old lyric, "I get by with a little help from my friends," some teens even perform oral sex as a favor for a friend.

If you are worried that such a casual view toward an act our grandmothers may never have heard of might be dangerous, some professionals aren't. J. Dennis Fortenberry, a physician who specializes in adolescent medicine, had these reassuring words for *USA Today*, "The fact that teenagers have oral sex doesn't upset me much from a public health perspective. From my perspective, relatively few teenagers only have oral sex. And so for the most part, oral sex, as for adults, is typically incorporated into a pattern of sexual behaviors that may vary depending upon the type of relationship and the timing of a relationship." What a relief! If my daughter is having oral sex with her boyfriend—or with her date, for that matter—I won't have to worry because she's probably doing other things as well!

Other professionals around the globe (and no doubt here as well) see the increase in oral sex as a positive development. A

2004 British newspaper article titled "Oral Sex Lessons to Cut Rates of Teenage Pregnancy," described how educators believe encouraging children to participate in oral sex is one effective way to curb teenage pregnancy and STD rates.

Newspapers in America took a cautious, amoral attitude about the CDCP study's results—ignoring the fact that our nation's rampant immorality has infected our children, and focusing on how such activities may infect them with diseases. But as one shrewd reporter pointed out, even if your moral standard is the risk of disease, statistics on American teen sexuality should be alarming.

Why? As the good doctor said, oral sex is not the only sexual activity among teens. The CDCP study found that almost the same number of teens having oral sex were having intercourse. And not only that. Few newspapers reported the uncomfortable details, but the study also found that anal sex is on the rise. This trend is serious from a health standpoint because according to earlier data released by the Center, anal sex is far more dangerous than other types: The probability of HIV acquisition by the receptive partner in unprotected oral sex with an HIV carrier is one per 10,000 acts. In vaginal sex, it's 10 per 10,000 acts. In anal sex, it's 50 per 10,000 acts. The reporter mentioned above had this to say:

> Do the math. Oral sex is 10 times safer than vaginal sex. Anal sex is five times more dangerous than vaginal sex and 50 times more dangerous than oral sex. Presumably, oral sex is far more frequent than anal sex. But are you confident it's 50 times more frequent?

As for the newspapers' omission of any facts regarding anal sex, he implies liberal politics may have played a role:

> If you live in Bergen County, N.J., congratulations. You get the only newspaper in the world that mentioned heterosexual anal sex, albeit briefly, in its write-up of the survey. Two other papers buried it in lines of statistics below their articles; the rest completely ignored it. Evidently anal sex is too icky to mention in print. But not too icky to have been tried by 35 percent of young women and 40 to 44 percent of young men—or to have killed some of them. . . . One in three women *admits* to having had anal sex by age 24. By ages 25 to 44, the percentages rise to 40 for men and 35 for women. And that's not counting the 3.7 percent of men aged 15 to 44 who've had anal sex with other men. . . . The spin that activists, scholars, and journalists have put on the survey—that abstinence-only sex education is driving teenagers to an epidemic of oral sex—doesn't hold up.

Faced with such unpleasant data, many parents in Middle America choose "not to know" what their kids are doing. Others know and do nothing. The price for such apathy may be the shattered spirits and bodies of their children.

SOS: SCHOOLS OVER-SEXED!

What do America's schools have to say about the extracurricular activities of their pupils? Are they taking the reins that parents have dropped to lead our children toward morality?

Individual teachers in our nation make heroic efforts, but taken as a whole, our education system has abandoned its stance as a moral gatekeeper in society. Or should I say changed its stance? After all, values are still taught. They are just the more modern kind. The main values spoken in class-rooms today are Moral Relativism, Safety, and that ultimate of all values, Tolerance. Schools today are progressive liberals' preferred forum for ripping anything that might even resem-ble morality or justice from the hearts and souls of today's children.

Generations of moral codes have become outdated, intole-rant nonsense. Instead of "honor your father and mother," chil-dren learn that their parents have been incorrectly conditioned in child rearing. ("Be sure to report your parents to the school guidance counselor if they lay one hand on you. It's for their own good.") Instead of being taught to behave themselves, chil-dren are given condoms and "safe sex" seminars.

And what do they learn at these seminars? Here are some mind-boggling examples of how public school administrators and teachers are molding your children into future productive citizens:

1) Planned Parenthood raised eyebrows by including instruc-tions to use Saran Wrap as protection when engaging in oral and anal sex in their recommended sex-education materials for eighth graders (a supplement during their ongoing battle for condom distribution, I suppose). The National Education Association (NEA), which represents public school teachers, has a section for sex education on its Web site with a link to the

Planned Parenthood site. (Never mind that poor kids trapped in failing schools are insulated from the prime condition that produces improvement: competition. At least they can have Saran Wrap!)

2) In April 2005, administrators of Brookline High School in Massachusetts distributed to hundreds of students a booklet entitled "The Little Black Book" without parental consent or notification. The booklet, written by the AIDS Action Committee, is really a "guide" to the pleasures of homosexual gratification. Included in the booklet are:

- Tips on coming out to friends and family

- How and where to meet other homosexuals

- A guide for drug usage including that of heroine and ecstasy (Not one statement against drug use is made in the entire booklet. In fact, the language sounds as though the authors are endorsing partying with illegal substances.)

- A guide on the "safety" aspects of various forms of gay sex

- A list of "Your Sexual Rights and Responsibilities" including this little gem: "You have the right to enjoy sex without shame or stigma!"

3) In Palmdale, California, elementary students were given a questionnaire containing sex-related questions without their

parents' permission or knowledge. The survey, given to kids aged seven to ten, included a section asking them to rate how often they experienced thoughts or emotions about:

- "Thinking about having sex"
- "Thinking about sex when I don't want to"
- "Washing myself because I feel dirty on the inside"
- "Touching my private parts too much"
- "Thinking about touching other people's private parts"
- "Not trusting people because they might want sex"
- "Getting scared or upset when I think about sex"
- "Having sex feelings in my body"
- "Can't stop thinking about sex"

Understandably outraged, a group of parents sued the school board, complaining that they would not have allowed their children to participate in the survey if they had known of the sexual nature of some of the questions. The 9th Circuit court ruled *against* the parents, rejecting their claims that they had been deprived of their fundamental right to "control the upbringing of their children by introducing them to matters of and relating to sex in accordance with their personal and religious values and beliefs." According to the all-wise judges, the parents' right to control their children was not "exclusive."

Taken all together, these anecdotes spell out a clear message from those running the show today in America's public schools: Move out of the way, Mom and Dad, Dr. Ruth has the floor!

READING, WRITING & HOMOSEXUALITY

Of all the agendas infiltrating education today, the homosexual platform has been the boldest and most successful. Marjorie King's 2003 article "Queering the Schools" exposes some of the many underhanded tactics activists use to advance the powerful homosexual movement in today's public schools. As a prime example of their methods she describes a GLSEN (Gay, Lesbian, Straight Education Network)-recommended resource manual distributed to all K-12 public schools in Saint Paul and Minneapolis:

> The manual presents an educational universe that filters everything through an LGBT [Lesbian, Gay, Bisexual, Trans-gendered] lens. Lesson ideas include "role playing" exercises to "counter harassment," where students pretend, say to be bisexual and hear hurtful words cast at them; testing students to see where their attitudes lie toward sexual "difference" (mere tolerance is unacceptable; much better is "admiration" and, best of all, "nurturance"); getting students to take a "Sexual Orientation Quiz"; and having heterosexual students learn 37 ways that heterosexuals are privileged in society.

King goes on to demonstrate that this "educational" agenda is not confined to the upper grades, but is a comprehensive plan to indoctrinate every child into the homosexual mindset:

> Nor is it ever too early to begin stamping out hetero-sexism. A 2002 GLSEN conference in Boston held a semi-nar on "Gender in the Early Childhood Classroom" that examined ways of setting "the tone for nontraditional gender role play" for *preschoolers*. To help get the LGBT message across to younger children, teachers can turn to an array of educational products, many of them available from GLSEN. Early readers include *One Dad, Two Dads, Brown Dad, Blue Dads*; *King and King*; and *Asha's Mums*.

While certain states have taken the lead, the educational goals of the homosexual movement in general and the GLSEN in particu-lar have tread inroads throughout the entire American land-scape. It won't surprise you that their prize pupil has been the state of California,

> where a new state law requires public schools to teach all K-12 students (and K means five-year-olds) "to appreci-ate various sexual orientations." What the new law might mean in practice, warned a state assemblyman, was on display at Santa Rosa High School, where invited homo-sexual activists "talked about using cellophane during group sex and said that 'clear is best because you can

see what you want to lick,'" or Hale Middle School in Los Angeles, where during an AIDS education course, "12-year-olds were subjected to graphic descriptions of anal sex and tips on how to dispose of condoms so parents don't find out."

Since most Americans link the lowest levels of morals to inner-city minorities and/or low-income neighborhoods fraught with crime and disease, I looked up Hale Middle School on the California Department of Education Web site to find out its student demographics. Surprise! Surprise! Hale Middle School is located in Woodland Hills, a very affluent city in northern Los Angeles County. Its high number of white students, 48 percent of the student body, dwarfs the overall district average of only 9 percent. What's more, the percentage of students who receive free or reduced price meals at Hale Middle School is substantially lower than the district, county, and state levels—about 40 percent of Hale students qualify compared to almost 77 percent for the LAUSD and nearly 62 percent for the county.

So where was the outrage from the privileged parents of Hale Middle School? Were they off somewhere polishing their BMWs, congratulating themselves on their open-minded tolerance? I escaped a life of drugs and poverty, and it angers me to find suburban, middle-class, white communities embracing the morals so often associated with the 'hood.

Will anyone speak out against the proliferation of GLSEN programs in America's schools? Not if surveys are correct. A recent Gallup poll shows that 54 percent of Americans today approve of homosexuals being elementary school teachers and

62 percent feel that they should be allowed to teach high school. If these poll participants represent a true cross-section of American culture, the majority of responders are white and middle class. They can't even be called "a bunch of liberals" either, since numbers show that while four out of ten Americans claim to be moderates and four claim to be conservative, only two say they are liberals. It seems that as more of our children today learn about Dick & Wayne, Middle America is nodding its approval.

Why are only a few people standing loudly and firmly for their conservative beliefs, especially when it involves the future of their children? Many parents have been hoodwinked. Like the overall progressive liberal agenda, the educational agenda of the far-left—especially that of gay activists—employs shrewd tactics in its mission to subvert traditional morality: 1) indoctrinate the principals and teachers, 2) keep the agenda quiet, 3) marginalize parental rights, and 4) marginalize those principles, teachers, and students who don't comply.

Don't think for one second that your child's school is protected. The underhanded tactics of the homosexual movement in the public school system, particularly those of the GLSEN, are extensive. For example, aware that most parents are concerned about safety, several radical activist groups have gained insider access into public schools in its name. Kevin Jennings, Executive Director of GLSEN, explains how they were able to penetrate Massachusetts's schools:

> We immediately seized upon the opponents' calling card—safety. . . . We knew that, confronted with real-life

stories of youth who had suffered from homophobia, our opponents would automatically be on the defensive. This allowed us to set the terms of the debate.

He goes on to describe the "great" strides of GLSEN over the last decade:

Today, ten years after we began our mission, more than twelve million students are protected by state laws. Nearly three thousand schools have GSAs or other student clubs that deal with LGBT issues. Over fifty national education and social justice organizations, including the National Education Association (NEA) have joined GLSEN in its work to create safe schools for our nation's children.

As a result of exploiting the safety issue, GLSEN has been able to pressure eight states to pass "safe school" laws protecting gay and lesbian students. Florida and New York, along with three other states, are considering similar legislation.

And what constitutes a "safe school"? A typical one has pink triangles above the doors of several classrooms to show that these rooms are a "safe" place for gays, lesbians, bisexuals, and trans-gendered students. Teachers are warned not to be critical of students' alternative lifestyle, but instead to encourage it. If any student dares to rebel against all this freedom, he is castigated for being intolerant—especially if his disapproval stems from religion. (And I thought liberals hated conformity.)

In actuality, "safe schools" are ones that intimidate any student or teacher who doesn't support the radical homosexual agenda of GLSEN, PFLAG (Parents and Friends of Lesbians and Gays), and other radical homosexual activist groups. Under the pretext of protecting homosexuals from being bullied, these extremists pursue their goal: to indoctrinate into our children the belief that everyone has the potential to become a homosexual.

Teachers are under intense scrutiny if they don't comply with the new tolerance regime. Legislation passed in California ensures that no one, even conscientious objectors, is exempt from homosexual indoctrination. After homosexual students in the town of Visalia complained of harassment, their district was punished with a federal court settlement under AB537 (a California safe school law) that forced teachers to receive mandatory gay-rights training. The following year, the district's ninth-grade students were scheduled to attend court-ordered classes taught by the GSA.

How's that for justice? While one wayward school is forced to submit to the propaganda of the GSA (Gay-Straight Alliance), schools across the nation ban students from wearing rebuttal T-shirts that dare to speak against homosexuality. For all their talk of tolerance, gay rights activists have anything but tolerance in mind. They want what they want, they want it now—and they will do anything to get it.

STDS IN AMERICA: WHEN DOING ANYTHING YOU PLEASE LEADS TO DISEASE

With the "anything goes" philosophy reigning in our televisions, music, and school systems, it should be no surprise that one in five Americans has a sexually transmitted disease. Yet despite our modern knowledge of STDs and the high numbers of infections, social resistance against abstinence programs remains intense.

It doesn't take a rocket scientist to understand that a person who abstains from sexual contact until marriage and who then remains faithful to an equally chaste spouse has an almost zero chance of contracting an STD. If nothing else, practicing this antiquated and prudish tradition invites no harm. Anyone promoting virginity or abstinence today, however, is greeted with smirks and labeled as primitive and intolerant.

The numbers surrounding the most deadly sexually transmitted disease, AIDS, unveil a society spinning out of control. In the year 2003, 18,017 of our citizens died from AIDS, bringing the cumulative total of AIDS deaths to 524,060. Tragic epidemics like this could be avoided if only Americans restrained their sexual behavior. Instead, standing firmly on the platform of unqualified tolerance, our culture has created a society of chaos . . . and death.

An examination of the health crisis we have created reveals that HIV/AIDS has migrated from the homosexual to the heterosexual community, and that today women account for 26 percent of newly diagnosed AIDS cases—quadruple the incidence among women in the 1980s. Black women compose over 70 percent of those cases, making AIDS the number one cause of death among African American women between the ages of twenty-five and forty-four.

Journalist Gwen Ifill jolted listeners of the 2004 debate between Vice President Cheney and John Edwards when she pointed out that "black women between twenty-five and forty-four are thirteen times more likely to die of the disease than their counterparts." Although health professionals are still trying to determine the precise channels through which the HIV virus is being transmitted to black women, drug use and sexual promiscuity are clearly contributing factors.

A recent *Newsweek* cover story helped bring more national attention to the HIV/AIDS epidemic among African American women. Unfortunately, its superficial and biased coverage was itself evidence of how such an educated, affluent country continues to propagate this disease. *Newsweek* left the false impression that:

- Traditional values, rather than being part of the solution to this problem, contribute to its cause;

- Men are helpless victims and responsibility lies exclusively with women;

- Choice and responsibility play a minimal role in sexual behavior;

- We can separate the HIV/AIDS problem from the general social and moral climate of our country.

A world in which females of any race can live a lifestyle of abstinence or marital monogamy is such a remote possibility to the *Newsweek* reporters that it did not receive a word of mention in the entire article. The only attention the reporters gave to traditional values was to claim that they make women submissive, and thus supposedly more prone to predatory male behavior. These modern sages also blamed traditional values for men's reluctance to discuss their homosexual behavior with the women they encounter.

Undeniably, many of the HIV instances appearing in black women can be traced back to the appallingly high percentage of black men who have done time in prison. Prisons are a breeding ground for homosexual behavior and HIV transmission, and when HIV positive men return home and engage in hetero-sexual sex, their partners are exposed. Even so, *Newsweek* reporters never discussed the relevance of transformative prison outreach programs such as Chuck Colson's, nor did they broach the sensitive area of screening prisoners for HIV before they are released. Once again, political correctness trumped absolute truth in the mainstream media.

SOUTHERN HOSPITALITY?

After hearing the high numbers of African American women infected with HIV, it is tempting for middle-class Americans to sigh in sympathetic disgust, shake their heads over the appalling lives of the "less fortunate," and tune back into the *O.C.* After all, most Americans living outside of metropolitan areas blame the last thirty years' decrease in morality on the people living in troubled inner-city neighborhoods.

But as I have already mentioned, if the most vulnerable in our society has moral pneumonia, then America as a whole has a moral cold. You may be surprised to know that the states with the greatest concentration of sexually transmitted diseases are located in the southeast portion of our country—the region known as the Bible Belt. For example, southern states have drastically higher rates of chlamydia than other regions. The following statistics suggest that some of that good old Southern hospitality may have crossed the line to immorality:

- Mississippi leads with 14.6% of women ages 15 to 44 who were tested in family planning clinics having the disease.

- Louisiana and Alabama follow with rates of 10.9 percent and 10 percent.

- The only state outside of the South with rates that compare to these is Rhode Island at 10.1 percent.

Other STDs such as gonorrhea and syphilis are most prevalent in southern and midwestern states:

- South Carolina, Mississippi, and Louisiana have the highest rates of gonorrhea, with each state reporting over 300 cases per 100,000 people.

- Tennessee has ten times the rate of syphilis as that of California, and South Carolina has well over three times the rate of gonorrhea than New York.

- Syphilis is so prevalent in this quadrant of the United States that it is almost an exclusively southern phenomenon.

Why is this happening in the South, a region known (and sometimes scorned) for honoring traditional morality? Yes, all humans make mistakes, and yes, a number of factors contribute to the South's high rate of STDs, including the level of education, use of contraceptives, and the availability of medical services. But still, you wouldn't expect an area of such biblical saturation to breed so many shameful infections. Not in a region where Judeo Christian morality has long been preached, whose residents make up the highest percentage of Americans who claim to adhere to some form of Christianity.

It is true most southerners have heard "Thou Shalt Not Commit Adultery" more than once in their lives, and that many can sing a bona fide gospel hymn. But they are not immune to the siren calls of our progressive society. The ugly scars from America's degeneration are not confined to the back alleys of Detroit or the Vegas strip joints. They are embedded in the rural fields of the Bible-thumpers as well.

GAY LIKE ME

Of all the changes in American morals in the past three decades, the most dramatic has been the integration of homosexuality into everyday American life. Little by little, the gay and lesbian agenda has invaded each public arena, most notably education, entertainment, and politics. Lifestyles once denounced as perverse by all but the fringes of society have maneuvered their way into the mainstream. Believe me, this assimilation was no accident.

Historians point to the 1969 Stonewall riots in New York City as the watershed moment when homosexuality in the United States came out of the proverbial closet. During the 1970s, while gays, lesbians, bisexuals, and transgendered people were celebrating their "freedom," homosexual activists begged the American public simply to tolerate them. Meanwhile, these same activists were developing a calculated strategy to force Americans not only to tolerate their lifestyle, but to endorse and applaud it.

The entertainment industry has played a mammoth role in the mainstreaming of homosexuals. Turn on most any show and you will find that the charming, nonthreatening homosexual friend of today has replaced the nosy housewife neighbor of yesterday. With the deliberate and clever integration of lovable gay caricatures and entertaining storylines, studio executives have opened the door for homosexuals to be welcomed into every American household.

Just take a look at NBC's *Will and Grace*, a television comedy series wildly popular with both audiences and critics. It features Grace Adler, a straight female interior decorator, who moves in with Will Truman, a hard-working, friendly gay lawyer. The other leading male character on the show is Will's friend, a flamboyant and silly homosexual man who garners most of the laughs. The two men play off of each other like Andy Taylor and Barney Fife in the 1960's *The Andy Griffith Show*, yet they are both homosexual. What an ingenious way to create a sense of "normalcy" for the gay lifestyle—baseball, apple pie, and a fuchsia boa with high heels!

Lest you think this indoctrination has been the natural progression of our illuminated society, remember that an active agenda has existed for decades to legitimize the homosexual lifestyle. Shockingly candid evidence of this agenda ran in *Christopher Street Magazine*, a revered gay rights magazine of

the late 1970s and early 1980s. Excerpts from its article outlin-
ing "Six Principles for the Persuasion of 'Straights'" reveal how
the public homosexual image has been shrewdly manipulated
and crafted:

1. The first order of business is desensitization of the
   American public concerning gays and gay rights.
   The principle behind this advice is simple: almost
   any behavior begins to look normal if you are
   exposed to enough of it. . . . The visual media . . .
   [is] a gateway into the private world of straights,
   through which a Trojan Horse might be passed. . . .
   The National Gay Task Force has had to cultivate
   quiet backroom liaisons with broadcast companies
   and newsrooms in order to make sure that issues
   important to the gay community receive some
   coverage.

2. Portray gays as victims, not as aggressive
   challengers. In any campaign to win over the
   public, gays must be cast as victims in need of
   protection so that straights will be inclined by
   reflex to assume the role of protector. . . . We must
   forego the temptation to strut our "gay pride"
   publicly whenever it conflicts with the Gay Victim
   image.

3. Our campaign should not demand direct support
   for homosexual practices, but should instead take
   anti-discrimination as its theme. *[Hence, the*

improper equating of racism with discrimination against homosexuality.]

4. Make gays look good. In order to make a Gay Victim sympathetic to straights you have to portray him as Everyman . . . the campaign should paint gays as superior pillars of society . . . in no time, a skillful and clever media campaign could have the gay community looking like the veritable fairy godmother to Western civilization.

5. Make the victimizers look bad. . . . To be blunt, they must be vilified . . . we intend to make the anti-gays look so nasty that average Americans will want to dissociate themselves from such types. *[And I thought all the gay-love floating around our nation was from our own innate kindness!]*

6. Solicit funds . . . those gays not supporting families usually have more discretionary income than average.

The homosexual movement's tactics have so cleverly seduced our society that it is nearly impossible for Middle America not to fall for its radical agenda, an agenda demanding many of us to surrender beliefs rooted in our families for generations. Honestly, what "bigot" today could disapprove of the sincere, savvy Will Truman or the funny, huggable Jack McFarland of *Will and Grace*? The duo-tyranny of the thought police and societal pressure has such a strong grip on American society that most of us today will not breathe a word in public against homosexuality for fear of being ostracized and maligned. (With friends like that, who needs hate crimes?)

"I PRONOUNCE YOU MAN AND . . . HUSBAND?"

An absolute endorsement by the list of "Who's Who" in America is not enough for the gay and lesbian movement. They want to overhaul the American family. In the past ten years, the battle over gay marriage has taken center stage in our culture. Cries for a national acceptance of gay marriage have been bolstered by sympathetic stories in the news media, liberal-voting regions across the country, and politicians who invent ways to circumvent the law.

Most Americans can recall when the mayor of San Francisco broke state law and began issuing "marriage" licenses to a few thousand homosexuals. His renegade antics were likely applauded in the state of Massachusetts, the only state that recognizes same-sex marriages. Others joining the gay parade are California, Connecticut, the District of Columbia, Hawaii, Maine, New Jersey and Vermont, all granting same-sex unions a similar legal status to civil marriage.

But in other areas of the country, such aggressive moral apathy struck a nerve. Nineteen states now have constitutional amendments explicitly barring the recognition of same-sex marriage, while even more have legal statutes defining marriage to two persons of the opposite sex. More ballot measures are pending, and all successful Defense of Marriage Acts have passed by considerable majorities, even in Oregon, a state where same-sex "marriage" proponents anticipated its defeat.

The fight isn't over, according to the National Gay and Lesbian Task Force. After Texas became the nineteenth state to overwhelmingly pass a constitutional amendment defending traditional marriage, Matt Foreman, the group's executive director said, "All that today's results show is that it is profoundly wrong and profoundly un-American to put the rights of a small minority of Americans up for a popular vote. This is not democracy; this is tyranny of the majority."

His accusing remarks were typical far-left spin. But unless Middle America stays on guard, the moral gains made by adopting these acts will mean nothing. True, a 2004 CBS poll revealed that over 73 percent of Americans are against the legal recognition of gay marriages. But there was a sharp difference in opinion among various segments of society. For example, strong opposition to gay marriage correlated with the level of religious attendance, older age, Republican Party affiliation, and residence in the southern states. African Americans also greatly favor a constitutional amendment defining marriage. On the other hand, levels of support for gay marriage were higher among the young, the nonchurchgoing, the Democratic-Party-affiliated, and those who lived in the western states and New England.

The most troubling pro-homosexual demographic from the survey—and the most telling about the shifting morals in our nation—was the young. While only 12 percent of those in the over sixty-five age bracket approved of gay marriage, a whopping 43 percent (the highest of any demographic surveyed) of those between the ages of eighteen and twenty-nine approved. These numbers reveal two things: first, that the homosexual indoctrination of our schools is working, and second, that America's future voting block may lean way toward the left.

Meanwhile, as Middle America breathes a sigh of relief that traditional marriage has crossed the first hurdle of state constitutional amendments (pressure for a federal marriage protection amendment still exists), many groups continue to actively fight for the legal recognition of same-sex marriage, including such Lesbian, Gay, Bisexual and Transgendered (LGBT) groups as HRC, Lambda Legal and NGLTF, and the issue-specific groups of Marriage Equality and Freedom to Marry.

For the time being at least, Americans continue to affirm the ideal of traditional marriage in the voting booths. But what about their daily lives? Do Middle Americans support marriage with their actions?

The National Marriage Project, a nonpartisan research institute at Rutgers University, recently released its annual study on the condition of marriage in America. The report found that not only does the United States lead the world in divorce rates—around 50 percent—but also that fewer Americans today are marrying than at any other time in recent history. Our nation's marriage rate has fallen by nearly 50 percent over the past three decades, and by 20 percent since 1995.

This marriage reduction doesn't mean passion is dead. Since 1960, the same year Mr. Moynihan wrote *The Negro Family: The Case for National Action*, unmarried cohabitation in the United States has increased by *1,200 percent*. Just as Moynihan warned Black America that it needs to change to prevent the deterioration of its society, voices of caution now speak to Middle America.

In an online article titled "Traditional marriage under fire: Who's really to blame?" conservative policy analyst Daniel Allot tells apathetic modern Americans that the reason for marriage's breakdown is neither legal nor political, but cultural. He discusses how, influenced by an invasive entertainment industry, American society has altered its view of matrimony from a "'til death do us part" commitment, to a self-serving, emotion-based "as long as it works" deal.

Allot argues that a generation of young Americans has grown up among evidence that traditional marriage does not work. He also points out that since same-sex marriage does not even exist in societies where marriages thrive, heterosexuals' trivial view towards marriage has catapulted activists' case for gay marriage.

Read his dead-on admonition:

Clearly, the key players in the battle over marriage are not politicians, judges or homosexual activists, but rather the millions of heterosexual couples who have thumbed their noses at marriage and abandoned the institution. . . . In the two-front war over marriage, the importance of opposing efforts to foist same-sex marriage on an unwilling public cannot be overstated. But, for those who truly care about the health of an institution that has been the bedrock of healthy families and societies for millennia, the push for same-sex marriage should also serve as a wake-up call as to just how fragile the institution has become at the hands of heterosexual couples. It is high time that the passion with which many Americans oppose same-sex marriage be matched with an equal amount of passion for the well-being of their own marriages.

―――――――――

We have come full circle to where I began my thoughts on the sexual state of America: the family. Certainly, the traditional American family is under siege, with the challenges for young parents never greater. The no-limits brand of freedom promoted in our country today—more aptly termed "license"—has sanctioned behaviors once considered abhorrent, abnormal, and deviant. As a result, we have seen crime rates skyrocket, sexually transmitted diseases multiply, and families crumble. In the name of "freedom," our permissiveness has brought upon us not the wrath of God, but the consequences of our own actions.

What is the cure for a society which has exchanged love and personal responsibility for lust and personal gratification? There is only one answer, and that is to reestablish our roots in personal responsibility and the traditional sense of right and wrong. Unless Middle America reins in our sexual lives and returns to decency, we will only sink further. We may find ourselves referring to these current, decadent times as "the good old days."

VICTIMIZATION IN THE GHETTO

Three jet airliners hijacked by Muslim extremists killed thousands of innocent victims in a few horror-filled minutes on September 11, 2001, waking up an apathetic America with its jolt. Suddenly, Old Glory appeared on a panorama of front porches and rear windows. Major news stories of yesterday faded into triviality. The bizarre scene of a unified Congress singing "God Bless America" on the Capitol steps felt natural. As though emerging a long period of slumber, our nation was again conscious of what it means to be an American. We were once again the *United* States, joined in our grief and outrage. Osama Bin Laden and his evil Al Qaeda, along with the dreaded Taliban of Afghanistan, became Public Enemy #1.

In time, life returned to almost-normal again. Americans outside of New York and D.C. resumed their daily lives. CNN added other stories to its lineup. And the righteous fury we had felt so strongly faded into distant resentment.

Then I heard it. I'm sure you did too, for all over national talk shows and broadcasts, an absurd theory arose from the "experts": *It was our fault.*

If only the United States hadn't done business with governments in the Middle East or taken any military action in that area . . . if only we weren't so biased towards Israel or greedy for oil . . . if only our Christian nation was not so intolerant of Islam—if only, if only, if only, then we would not have incited these terrorists.

With the blame came the excuses . . . for the terrorists. After all, the murderers were victims too. Victims of religious fanaticism, of poverty, and, according to the socialists among us, victims of the evils of imperialistic capitalism. As enlightened citizens of the millenium, (violin strings, please) we should view their misguided zeal as the cry for help of a desperate, humiliated people, the bottled-up frustration of a band of backward countries that had been much defeated in the marketplace and battlefield.

A TERRORIST IS A TERRORIST

We should have seen such upside-down reasoning coming. After all, the old Flip Wilson con "The devil made me do it" has evolved into the more politically correct "My genes (or upbringing) made me do it." We live in a nation of insanity pleas, self-help groups, and tobacco lawsuits, whose notions of justice come from the latest episode of *Law and Order*. Liberals with the gall to blame our country for 9/11 could choose no better forum for their blather.

One such libertarian, University of Colorado professor Ward Churchill, took his "scholarly" position to the point of lunacy by exonerating the terrorists and laying the blame on the victims of 9/11. His rationale? U.S. foreign policy has driven the normally peaceful, even docile, Muslims to commit treacherous acts of murder. They had no choice; they were forced to retaliate against so-called violent acts perpetuated by the U.S. government in Middle Eastern countries. As for blaming the everyday Americans working inside the World Trade Center, read his own words:

True enough, they were civilians of a sort. But innocent? Gimme a break. They formed a technocratic corps at the very heart of America's global financial empire, the "mighty engine of profit" to which the military dimension of U.S. policy has always been enslaved, and they did so both willingly and knowingly. [The victims in the World Trade Center buildings were] too busy braying, incessantly and self-importantly, into their cell phones, arranging power lunches and stock transactions, each of which translated, conveniently out of sight, mind and smelling distance, into the starved and rotting flesh of infants. If there was a better, more effective, or in fact any other way of visiting some penalty befitting their participation upon the little Eichmanns inhabiting the sterile sanctuary of the twin towers, I'd really be interested in hearing about it.

And we worry about rappers polluting the public airways? This tenured academic spews his vitriol in college classrooms.

Seven months after these infamous words of Professor Churchill, the mayor of London, Ken Livingstone, announced that the reason for the mass transit bombings in London was Western intervention in the Middle East since World War I. Prime Minister Tony Blair offered no such nonsense at the press conference immediately following the attack. But he did go overboard in his efforts not to use the word "Islamic" to describe terrorism when discussing the tragedy. (Perhaps he wanted to pursue leads on the Dutch, the Swedes, or the Quaker Liberation Organization.)

Despite Blair's toe-stepping, even the most news-ignorant American knew exactly who was to blame: radical Islamic terrorists. I was pleasantly surprised to see the *Dallas Morning News* buck the PC system by declaring to its readers that it would no longer call the perpetrators of these horrific crimes against humanity in Iraq or elsewhere "insurgents" because they were indeed terrorists that blatantly and haughtily kill unarmed men, women, and children. At last, a media outlet that wasn't afraid to call a spade a *spade,* or a terrorist a *terrorist.* (Then again, Texas was its own republic at one point.)

Blair, on the other hand, qualified his statements about Islam even before British intelligence and the CIA had determined responsibility. Why? Because he did not want to "offend" any followers of Islam, especially those living in his own country, or the legions of voters who'd taken up their "cause." On a deeper level, Tony Blair was trying to make a distinction that is impossible to make: For it is the teachings of Islam, no matter how twisted the interpretation may be, which these terrorists use to justify their actions. They believe that they are fulfilling the will of Allah by fighting against Western corruption and excess, and that by doing so, they will receive reward in heaven.

How else do you explain that Islamic terrorists over the years have come from almost every Middle Eastern country that claims Islam as its national religion—Turkey, Syria, Afghanistan, Libya, Jordan, Egypt? Or the lack of overwhelming condemnation by these same countries against the actions of Osama Bin Laden and Al Qaeda after the first and second World Trade Center attacks, the attacks on Madrid, and the many others? In several of these countries, terrorism is a state-sponsored government project. Whether Tony Blair will admit it or not, there is a direct link between Islam and radical Muslim terrorists.

As for London's mayor, Ken Livingstone, and our own Professor Churchill, I suppose they will have much to discuss when they're both invited to appear on the *Surreal Life*. Incidentally, neither of these men lost their jobs for voicing such treasonous statements. In the general public, their remarks barely made a ripple. Middle America and England were too busy being tolerant to notice.

DENY, DENY, DENY (WHEN FICTION REPLACES TRUTH)

One of the main complaints in recent years has been about how Bush's foreign policy is alienating us from the rest of the world—even Europe. It seems many in our country care more about winning the congeniality award than they do about protecting our national security. I wonder if all the image-conscious among us would truly want to "go European" if they understood the mode of thinking there.

Our response to 9/11, terrorism, and Iraq compared to the responses of France, Russia, and Germany reveals the radical differences in our perceptions of morality. For a prime example of French popular opinion and of their loathing of the United States, check out the number-one bestselling book in France in the summer of 2002: *The Horrifying Fraud* by Thierry Meyssan. This literary gem claims that it was in fact the U.S. military that bombed the Pentagon, and not a terrorist-hijacked plane. (You can imagine all the reasons we'd want to bomb our own country.) While this theory has been peddled by fringe-left journalists trying to make a buck in both the U.S. and Europe, what makes Meyssan's book particularly notorious is that the French read it as the gospel truth—even though Meyssan's typical fare is on the level of the *Enquirer*. He is just as likely to write a book on alien autopsies as on war theories. CNN's Jim Bittermann described some of the man's compelling evidence and credentials:

> Although he did not personally travel to the U.S. for his research and does not claim to be an expert, Meyssan bases his theory—and now a follow-up book defending his theory—on his own analysis of official documents. He also uses photographs which he says do not show much that look like an airplane . . . But photographs Meyssan left out . . . picture debris that clearly came from the hijacked plane.

A self-professed non-expert analyzes official documents and purposely omits pictures that contradict his claims. Quite a reliable source! Yet, the French believe Meyssan, buying over 200,000 copies of his propaganda in the summer of 2002 rather than accepting the word of trusted allies.

The United States' response to the tragic events of 9/11, the Taliban of Afghanistan, and Saddam Hussein has been remarkably courageous. While most "civilized" countries of the United Nations would rather negotiate with the killers than stand up, hunt them down, and bring them to justice (after all, they had a hard childhood), Bush knew that the lives of three thousand innocent people, the true victims of 9/11, demanded that something be done.

VICTIMS 'R' US

The United States may be tough on international terrorists, but we take a gentler approach with our own criminals. In an atmosphere severely lacking in personal responsibility, we neither recognize evil for what it is nor hold evildoers accountable. This mindset allows liberals to blame everyone and everything except the criminals themselves for terrorism and/or good old-fashioned murder. For instance, modern criminologists and detectives have come to the conclusion that serial killers are the result of genetic and biological factors. A man murders ten people? He must have elevated levels of testosterone, an extra chromosome, or a brain defect! A teenager shoots up his high school? He must have been physically abused. Certainly a variety of factors play a role in the overall outcome of one's life, but they cannot excuse a person for his or her actions.

Exemplifying today's twisted thinking, Lionel Dahmer, father of the infamous Jeffrey Dahmer, lays the blame for his son's murderous actions at the feet of his son's mother. He claims that her psychosomatic illnesses and erratic behavior were behind Jeffrey's killing spree. Certainly not poor Jeffrey—he is only the pitiable result of hormonal imbalances and a nutty fruitcake of a mother. That must mean Jeffrey's *mother* was actually the one responsible for those thirteen murders. And what about *her* parents? You get the picture.

While the Moderate Middle attends to their portfolios, liberal legalism has bolstered up pleas of insanity for criminals to avoid personal responsibility. In 2004, a teacher was charged with several counts of sexual misconduct with a fourteen-year-old student. Debra LaFave pleaded not-guilty-by-reason-of-insanity to having sex with the boy in a portable classroom, in her own house, and in the back of a car. My response to this plea? No kidding! Anyone would have to be "insane" to put her marriage, career, and freedom on the line for a tryst with a middle-school student. But a lapse in sanity does not negate her accountability.

Do you remember the horrific story of Lorena Bobbitt? In the early 1990s, she was acquitted of charges of mutilating her husband's genitalia. While he was sleeping, she cut off her husband's penis with a carving knife. Her reason? He was "selfish" with regards to their marriage bed. She also claimed he had sexually abused her, a charge of which he was later acquitted. Amazingly the jury found her not guilty after she pleaded not guilty because of insanity. They apparently believed that she had reacted out of an "irresistible impulse" to maim her husband, and therefore should not be held liable for her actions. In the end, Lorena was not a woman who maimed a man—she was the victim of a chemical meltdown!

Criminals aren't the only ones who have jumped on the victim train. I can remember when it was en vogue in the 1990s for many celebrities to blame everyone, especially their parents, for their abuse of alcohol and drugs and other generally slovenly behavior. Some even underwent therapy and then "remembered" abuse from their past. (One celebrity victim was Roseanne Barr, whose sexual abuse allegations against her parents eventually proved false.) Following the lead of our cultural elite, millions of Americans took to the therapist's couch. Although some had genuinely tragic pasts, others, hypnotized by sympathetic (and profiting) psychologists, manufactured tales of abuse and discrimination. It seems false victimization is good for the imagination.

Workers in the field of mental health do a valuable service for our broken human race, but those who encourage their patients to embrace victimhood are doing them no favor. When a person disavows himself from personal responsibility, he may lose some pressure and obligations, but he also loses dignity and personal integrity. In their absence, he seeks out other avenues to appease his base desires for comfort, money, and power. For example, consider the most popular type of entertainment for young black Americans: rap music. Its raw images and lyrics, so offensive to middle-class Americans, are evidence that kids have digested popular culture's message of "no wrongs" and "my rights." And we can't forget the suburban appeal of Showtime's cutting-edge (translation: vulgar, politically progressive, and/or offensive) show *Weeds*. It portrays the life of a recently-widowed white middle-class mom who sells marijuana to pay the bills. Its message to Middle America? *Yeah, she's selling drugs, but the poor woman has to do something to make it in this tough economy!* If the ultimate values in the ghettos and suburbs of our country are acquisition and power, it doesn't matter how a person attains them. Dealing drugs is as reasonable a way as getting an MBA.

NOW: NATIONAL ORGANIZATION OF WHINERS

In a politically-correct society rife with victims, the principal victim is integrity. Dr. Lawrence Summers stumbled into this lesson at an economics conference dealing with diversity shortly after taking his prestigious new position as president of Harvard University. Speaking informally, Summers suggested that one possible reason fewer women were on science and engineering faculties might be that women have less inherent ability to perform at the highest levels of these fields.

Is this theory possible? Yes. Can you say it at a liberal university? Apparently not. Summers' remarks provoked the wrath of many members of the Harvard faculty. Far from rigorously examining his hypothesis (aren't universities supposed to pursue knowledge?), their first reactions were to attack Summers, force an apology, and demand politically-motivated action. To no one's surprise, Harvard soon had a new task force to recommend procedures for hiring more women.

If the Harvard faculty had been more interested in truth than politics, they could have convened an inquiry into the proposition that women may not be as genetically disposed to math and science as men. If the inquiry found such a theory might be possible—not that it *is the case*, but that it *might be possible*, which is what Summers suggested—then the faculty that attacked him could be fired. If results showed that the theory was not a possibility, then Summers could be fired.

My guess is that Summers would submit to such an exercise, and that the dissenting faculty members would not. They would not because they know they would lose. Evidently, careful courageous inquiry is not what interests them. Their concern is to advance their preconceived notions about how the world should be.

Incidentally, what if Summers had said he simply had no idea why there are fewer women on science faculties? Or suppose he had suggested the phenomenon was impossible to understand. These responses also would have been unacceptable. The only acceptable response for protestors was one politically-charged magic word: *Discrimination.*

Discrimination is the rallying cry of numerous "victim" groups demanding protection from Washington, D.C. and from state and local governments. For their part, feminist organizations claim that male dominance is so engrained in the fabric of our society that nothing less than federal legislation will do to rid our culture of such "treachery." Take a look at this excerpt from the "About" section found on the Web site for the National Organization for Women (NOW):

> Since its founding in 1966, NOW's goal has been to take action to bring about equality for all women. NOW works to eliminate discrimination and harassment in the workplace, schools, the justice system, and all other sectors of society; secure abortion, birth control and reproductive rights for all women; end all forms of violence against women; eradicate racism, sexism and homophobia; and promote equality and justice in our society.

In what fantasyland are they living?

Taking the defensive posture of "victim," they talk as though discrimination against women is so commonplace that only men can get a decent job. Yet this is simply not true. Women today have more control over their lives, have greater accessibility to education, and have greater power and influence in the workforce than ever. Claiming victim status is just a ploy to garner more power for the NOW agenda: to control reproduction by any means necessary.

The women's movement is another demographic of American society waving the "victim" sign. What began as a campaign to stop the stereotyping and objectifying of women has, like many government programs, evolved into quotas—quotas which treat people like objects, by the way. As do generalizations that correlate earnings to gender. Dehumanization is fine as long as it produces politically acceptable results.

The idea of quotas brings to mind a discussion from my previous book, *Uncle Sam's Plantation*, about the meaninglessness of the term *minority*. After all, what is a minority? It obviously has nothing to do with numbers. There are certainly ethnic groups in our nation with fewer numbers than blacks or Hispanics who are not considered minorities. (Ever heard of discrimination against America's Croatians?) Furthermore, no other group except blacks has ancestors who were dragged here in chains and enslaved, so that isn't a necessary qualification. Clearly, the term *minority* cannot be defined because it is a political label used exclusively for political purposes. These purposes, with all sorts of attempts at special treatment, wind up producing the same dehumanization that advocates claim to combat.

This former welfare mother has news that may disappoint those who think that the ultimate revenge against the evil majority and their neighbor's new Hummer is that their kid got into Harvard: No ultimate political solution can make our world a better or more just place. No matter how many rallies we attend or resolutions we pass, people will always have different levels of talent and ability. Some will inevitably come into this world "a step ahead." The challenge for us all is to accept our own strengths and weaknesses, give other people the same grace we would hope to be given, and then accept life in a world that will never be completely, 100-percent fair. Trying to make sure that every person starts and ends on the same page is not only foolish, but impossible.

Nevertheless, decades of liberal propaganda have seduced millions of Americans into believing that they are owed something, that someone else is at fault for their problems, and that the federal government had better do something about it—or else. Categorizing and labeling these victim groups allows liberal politicians to gain ideological control over group members. Rather than being considered individuals with a unique set of circumstances (as we all are), now they are members of a group that has only one identifying characteristic—black or female or short or handicap—you name it. For every human characteristic other than "white male," there is a victim group looking for someone to sympathize with their "plight." In fact, with the vast array of quotas and interest groups in existence, today's white males should claim entitlement. Move over Norwegian left-handed lesbians and height-challenged, smoking vegetarians, save some sympathy for the middle-class heterosexual white male!

GAY BUT NOT HAPPY

Some groups buy the lie that they are first-and-foremost victims. Other groups choose to lie. As the politics of control gained momentum among African Americans in the 1970s, other groups began to seek "victim" status and the benefits due them. One of the most hypocritical of these groups is the loosely confederated AIDS coalition.

When the first cases of AIDS were reported in Laguna Beach, San Francisco, and Fire Island, no one knew or understood the disease. They did, however, know that it was radically affecting their licentious lifestyle. At the onset of the epidemic, homosexuals tried to downplay the significance of this fatal disease so as not to inhibit the sexual behavior of the local gay community. As the disease spread, instead of considering their perversions as the root cause of the health crisis, AIDS activists began blaming Presidents Ronald Reagan and George W. Bush for the dramatic rise in HIV infections and AIDS cases in the United States.

AIDS activism often tends toward the extreme, with some protests resulting in violence. Think about it: cancer and heart disease organizations don't employ the same radical tactics to get their message out. I recently watched a television show called *The Black Forum* where three guests tried to explain the prevalence of AIDS in the black community, especially among black males. Not one of them stated that it had anything to do with a lack of traditional morality or self-control. No one pointed out that (according to a 2003 report) over 577,300 black men between the ages of 20–39—nearly 10 percent of black males in their twenties—were incarcerated. They didn't discuss how nearly 5 percent of all black men inhabit a prison system rife with homosexual activity and HIV. Instead, in the usual liberal mindset, they blamed the high AIDS numbers on various "propaganda" from conservative groups, especially the Reagan administration.

The various civil rights acts over the last century, along with numerous court decisions, have done much to ensure that all citizens of the United States are able to enjoy the same freedoms without fear of violence or discrimination. However, that movement has since morphed into one that seeks to protect not only individual *rights*, but also individual *behavior*. Victimization replaced racism as the driving force of the movement, and other "minority" groups literally came out of the closet to claim that their civil rights had been violated through years of institutional repression.

The formerly race-only cause of civil rights soon welcomed abortion advocates, homosexual activists, the handicapped, and even animals into the same category. Yes, even now radical environmentalists are decrying the evils of "specieism," claiming that the civil rights of animals have been violated by a human species that sees itself as superior to all others in the animal and plant kingdoms. Yesterday our country freed the slaves, today it saves the whales.

Assuming the role of victim and playing upon the sympathies and fears of a nation living in the "not-wanting-to-offend-anyone" mode, radical feminists and homosexuals made tremendous inroads into Middle America during the 1980s and 1990s by claiming that their inherent sex and sexual orientation granted them special rights under the law.

Beginning with the Stonewall riots of 1969, homosexuals demanded that their brand of sexual promiscuity be protected by state and federal laws. At the time, most states had statutes against sodomy, especially sex between two men or two women. Utilizing the ongoing civil rights movement, gay activists began claiming that their sexual desires were inherent and immutable. Many said that they had been born that way and that trying to change to heterosexuality was only a vain attempt at normalcy.

In the early 1990s, it was "discovered" that homosexuals were, in fact, genetically or biologically predisposed toward their sexual desires. So-called research tried to identify a "gay" gene, and many homosexual advocates were soon spreading the glorious news that the inherent trait of "gayness" had been discovered and that homosexuals comprised 10 percent of the population. With this propaganda, the homosexual movement soon began riding the coattails of civil rights. Gay men and women compared themselves to black Americans by stating that both groups were in the same fight for civil rights.

Their earnest campaign, propelled by the sympathetic entertainment industry with movies like *Philadelphia,* proclaimed that homosexual orientation was a genetic trait related to the structure of the brain, and thus these discriminated-against individuals deserved to be protected from all the homophobic, intolerant bigots (anyone who disagrees with the gay lifestyle) out there.

And Middle America bought it. Choosing to root for the team whose star players include Elton John, Ellen DeGeneres, Melissa Etheridge, and Rosie O'Donnell, many moderate Americans happily discarded the cumbersome traditional morality they had grown up with and embraced the sexy "new" pseudo-morality of relativism.

Few converts gave any thought to the circumstances and motivation behind the It's-Natural-To-Be-Gay movement. For example, many Americans cite both the American Psychological Association's (APA) and the American Psychiatric Association's (APA) normalization of homosexuality as evidence that gay men and women are not to be stigmatized or considered immoral in their behavior. However, few understand that the events surrounding the APAs' decision-making process were less than scientific or unbiased. Rather, in 1973, homosexual groups put a tremendous amount of pressure upon both APAs and essentially coerced the doctors representing these groups to change their policies.

The truth is, the argument that homosexuality is biological in nature, and therefore deserving of civil rights protection, is completely off base with reality. Yesterday's so-called ground-breaking research has now been debunked, and pro-gay science discredited. Back then, Simon LeVay supposedly produced evidence that homosexuality and homosexual tendencies could be linked to brain structure. But LeVay's methods have since been proven to be not just unreliable, but completely flawed. Evidence of a "gay" gene has also been found to lack any real credence, and the much publicized "10 percent homosexual" statistic was skewed from the start.

Without a genetic and/or biological link to sexual orientation, one cannot equate the condition of homosexuality to the inherent quality of race. Race is innate; homosexuality is not. Since sodomy is not inherent, the equating of homosexual behavior and homosexual marriage to a civil rights issue is without basis. Famed writer and historian Shelby Steele refuted the idea of homosexual marriage as a struggle for civil rights protection in an essay for the *Wall Street Journal*:

> But gay marriage is simply not a civil rights issue. It is not a struggle for freedom. It is a struggle of already free people for complete social acceptance and the sense of normalcy that follows thereof—a struggle for the eradication of the homosexual stigma.

Even so, most Americans have absorbed the sensational snippets the media has presented over the years portraying homosexuals as being products of genetics and biology. Evidence found contrary to the homosexual agenda rarely if ever appears in the major news outlets—no front-page retractions or explanatory bold headlines. Hence an entire nation has been duped. Misinformation and propaganda have convinced many in Middle America that sodomy deserves to be protected by the same civil rights language and legislation that protects blacks.

AFRICAN AMERICANS: A RACE OF VICTIMS

Just as many American minds hold false facts regarding homosexuality, several will retain the highly exaggerated number of deaths relayed by rain-soaked reporters regurgitating horrific accounts of anarchy and murder in New Orleans during 2005's Hurricane Katrina: an estimated ten thousand. By the time the much less sensationalized and sharply reduced true numbers came out, most Americans had turned off their television sets. Nevertheless, one thing was clear: the city of New Orleans was brimming over with thousands of seemingly helpless blacks. Picture after picture of the storm's victims solidified our nation's image of urban African Americans as a forgotten, impoverished, degenerate culture. Cries of racism grew louder.

However, the worst thing that has happened to black Americans over the past forty years is not racism, although you could point to specific incidences to try and argue that. An astute observer will notice that racism is only a veneer covering something much more destructive and pervasive. The real detriment to African Americans has been the adoption of the victim mentality by a majority of the black culture.

St. John Chrysostom states "that the events of this life in themselves are indifferent matters and take on the character of good and evil for us according to our response to them." In other words, racism is not as much of the problem as our response to prejudice and discrimination is. For whites, that response has largely been to ignore prejudice when they see or hear it, especially among their peers or in their own family. For blacks, the overwhelming response to racism has been to define ourselves by it.

Look at African Americans living in the early part of this century. Many prospered in the midst of extreme racial hatred. Instead of responding to that hatred with a "woe is me" attitude, many fought harder and achieved both respect and success. Through the years, black American citizens like George Washington Carver, Booker T. Washington, Jackie Robinson, Louis Armstrong, Ben Carson, Richard Parsons, and

Condoleezza Rice refused to define themselves according to the prejudice surrounding them.

But courage like that is difficult and rare. It is much easier to believe the hatred around you, live out low expectations, and blame others for your situation in life. That is why those who choose truth over finger-pointing in the black culture are in the minority. The few who take the high road will tell you that if anything has retarded individual and corporate black growth, it is the fact that so many African Americans have sought and still seek to lay the blame for their problems at the feet of others, namely white America.

(Some of you balk at this idea and will immediately dismiss what I'm about to tell you. That is because you've been conditioned by liberals whose only goal in life is to determine the parameters of society and then make sure that they corral you into one of their preconceived barnyard pens. Remember *Animal Farm*? As long as you remain in that pigpen, you're OK. But the minute you step foot outside, the thought police are there to bully you back into place. If I had lived in Soviet Russia, I would be in a gulag by now.)

The victim mentality has plagued the black community and the nation as a whole for several decades now, and its sway over the minds of generations has not only corrupted hearts and minds, but also stifled countless individuals' ability to succeed. To better grasp the problem, think of it in terms of red-headed "Samantha." If Samantha receives consistently poor job evaluations, she has a few options. One option is to take an honest look at herself and decide what she needs to change in her life. Perhaps she needs to go back to college and complete her

Associate's or Bachelor's degree. Maybe she needs to manage her time more effectively or develop a more professional attitude in her relationship with her peers or boss. Whatever the need, Samantha will greatly improve her chances for success by looking inside herself for the source of her problem and then making the necessary adjustments.

However, if Samantha listens to the propaganda of the Left, she will decide that the real problem is that her boss is out to get her or that her peers don't like redheads. As a result, she will only develop more and more reasons for not accomplishing the tasks found in her job description. Over time, she will become overly defensive even though she has no real evidence to support her claims. The real reason for her problems will plague her daily life no matter how many different jobs she tries. By taking on the identity of "victim," Samantha will forever be stumbling in the dark and blaming someone else that she didn't bring a flashlight.

This has been the situation of the black community ever since President Lyndon Johnson caved to political pressures and introduced his Great Society. For over forty years, black America has seen itself as the victim of white prejudice and discrimination. And this is no wonder, because blacks have had a terrible history of enslavement, torture, and murder. To state that African Americans have not been victims is to simply deny the facts.

But there is a major difference between being a victim and living in the victim mentality. The victim understands that cruelties have been committed against him. He may even mourn for what might have been. But rather than wallow in self-pity, he gets up, brushes himself off, and seeks to move on with his life.

Other true victims in life—rape victims, sufferers from child abuse, survivors of the Holocaust and other atrocities—face the same decision: No matter how horribly they have suffered or how justified their anger toward those who have harmed them, they will either define themselves by that abuse or by the fact that God has created them as a unique human being with special abilities. One road leads to hope and opportunities; the other leads to bitter stagnation.

A victim realizes that obstacles are to be expected, that life is not fair. Knowing this, he can deal with each day's obstacle as it comes. And if he fails to keep his promises, if he doesn't show up to work on time—if he sins—he is the first to admit that it is his fault. The person living with the victim mentality, however, sees every problem, every failure, as the direct result of someone else's actions. Because of our history, black Americans have had valid reason to point to the white community for our dire straits. But after forty years of welfare, affirmative action, and preferential treatment—combined with the fact that white racism has subsided dramatically since the 1960s—African Americans can no longer blame others for their state in life.

Sadly, black America's victim mentality has only perpetuated a growing problem of crime, disease, and illiteracy. Bill Cosby explained this when he said that the problems facing inner-city minority neighborhoods were the direct result of the members of those communities not taking personal responsibility for their actions:

> It is almost analgesic to talk about what the white man is doing against us, and it keeps a person frozen in their

seat. It keeps you frozen in your hold that you are sitting in to point up and say, "That's the reason why I am here." We need to stop this. . . .

Why is it so hard for black America to move on? Hoover Institute's Shelby Steele believes that part of the reason the black community clings to the victim mentality rather than face the challenges of life with dignity is because of "race-holding":

> Race-holding allows a black to retreat into his racial identity as an excuse for not using his talents to the fullest out of fear that he really cannot compete . . . I think they choose to believe in their inferiority, not to fulfill society's prophecy about them, but for the comforts and rationalizations their racial 'inferiority' affords them. They hold their race to evade individual responsibility. The margin of choice scares them, as it does all people.

By hiding under the cover of "inferiority," many blacks are able to retreat from the real world of competition and risk. Whether or not an individual African American is able to compete with other races in an integrated marketplace instead of within the conclaves that many African Americans have built for themselves is uncertain. Stepping off Uncle Sam's Plantation and running headlong into trials and adversities provides for a tremendous amount of uncertainty, something most Americans of every race are less and less willing to incorporate into their daily lives. Black Americans, therefore, retreat to the one thing that is assumed to be certain—inferiority and the sympathetic gestures which that "status" provides.

John McWhorter explains this attitude in detail in his book *Authentically Black*. He says:

> Black Americans have been so uniquely susceptible to this ideology because it offers a balm for something sitting at the heart of the African American consciousness: a sense that at the end of the day, black people are inferior to whites. Certainly on the surface we hear incessantly about black pride. But lying below this is a sad historical legacy: an internalization of the contempt that the dominant class once held us in, and sometimes still does. . . . This is a tragedy. . . . All the black Americans out there grousing about "white supremacy" and smugly dismissing "black conservatives" as naïve sellouts are speaking from this private sense of inadequacy. *No one who misses this can fully understand the race problem in modern America.*

If victimization is the trigger of the gun that black culture holds to its head, then the belief that racism is overly prevalent in American society is the finger that pulls that trigger. African Americans have been deluded into believing that the root cause to every one of their difficulties can be traced to white racism.

The reason for low test scores on standardized achievement tests? White schools have been given preferential treatment in terms of funding. The reason for the disproportionately high number of black inmates in federal and state prisons? Judges, juries, and law-enforcement officials have actively sought out African Americans as their primary targets. The reason for the extremely high rate of AIDS in the black community? The U.S. government manufactured the virus in a laboratory for the express purpose of destroying millions of "undesirable" African Americans.

The conspiracy-theory syndrome of a person suffering from the victim mentality looks for all kinds of bizarre evidence to support his claims. If I've decided you are the reason for all my problems, it's pretty easy to be suspect of any action or non-action you make towards me. Delusion rules the day. Sadly, it often results in defiance to anything resembling truth and wisdom. In the end, the person is left in a state of self-imposed bondage from which no one can free him.

A TALE OF TWO RIOTS

In 1992, the Los Angeles riots brought three days of death and destruction to the city's downtown neighborhoods. Enraged by the news that four white police officers had been acquitted in the beating case of Rodney King, thousands of people took to the streets in the late afternoon hours of April 29th and began ripping motorists from their cars, lighting buildings on fire, and wreaking havoc across the city.

A large percentage of those causing the violence were black and were using the verdicts as an excuse to steal and create general pandemonium. I was shocked to witness people breaking into the same stores they had just shopped in hours earlier. Many of the looters knew the store owners on a first-name basis. I myself felt the wrath of the looters as my own business suffered the violence of thugs and street gangs. In the end, over fifty people were killed and another three thousand were injured. Estimates of the total damage were between $800 million and $1 billion.

Beneath the shock and horror Middle America expressed over the events, many were saying, "I'm not surprised." Black America saw their situation as hopeless and most white Americans agreed. (Ever hear of the tyranny of low expectations?) Whether they viewed the violence as the inevitable eruption of an oppressed people, or fumed over the mayhem of those "thugs in the 'hood," few middle-class Americans were surprised to see inner-city blacks behaving so.

I bet few citizens had heard of the Tulsa race riots of 1921. At that time, north Tulsa, known as the Greenwood district, was predominantly black and extremely prosperous. Of course, prosperity among blacks in a predominantly white state only fueled racial tensions because of white jealousy and envy.

On May 31 of that year, Dick Rowland, a black man who shined shoes for a living, stepped onto an elevator operated by a white woman known as Sarah Page. Reports are conflicting, but apparently Rowland stepped on Page's foot and, as she was about to lose her balance, reached out to prevent her from falling. Since there were no witnesses, rumors spread that Rowland had attempted to assault or molest Page, and he was quickly arrested.

With racism already prevalent in the city (Tulsa had a KKK office in one of its downtown buildings), whites called for the lynching of Rowland and began to gather outside of the Tulsa county courthouse where he was jailed. To protect Rowland, approximately seventy-five armed blacks, many of whom were World War I veterans, also gathered outside the courthouse. In a brief struggle between a black man and a white man, a gun was discharged and the white man was shot dead. In a flash, the deadliest race riot in American history was on.

Blacks hurriedly organized themselves in defense of their Greenwood homes and businesses, but to no avail. Over the course of two days, the thirty-five blocks of the Greenwood district were burned to the ground by white rioters who sought to exact their vengeance on their black neighbors. The first official report said that ten whites and twenty-six blacks had been killed, but recent investigations reveal that upwards of three hundred people lost their lives.

A comparison of the two riots reveals how blaming others for our struggles has brought African Americans backward instead of forward. Yes, both riots were centered on the issue of race, and as with any race conflict, the struggle for equality was palpable. But there is something strikingly different about the Los Angeles riots compared to the one in Tulsa. In the Los Angeles riots, groups of predominantly black and Hispanic men attacked, beat, and murdered several other people (mostly minorities) throughout the city. The excuse for their behavior was that they were simply reacting to the non-guilty verdicts of the four white police officers. (I'm not here to question the veracity of the court's decision or to address the anger of blacks the day of the verdict. For the record, I'm of the opinion that those four police officers were guilty and deserved to be stripped of their authority to work in law enforcement in Los Angeles or anywhere else for that matter.)

The Tulsa riot, on the other hand, was the result of white racists who wanted to take their frustrations of jealousy out on the most convenient victims available. The blacks involved in the riot were doing what anyone under attack would do— organizing a defense of their families or fleeing to the nearby Osage hill country. In the Tulsa riot, the whites were the perpetrators; in Los Angeles, it was the blacks.

But besides the different colors of the instigators, something else was different between the Tulsa and Los Angeles rioters. Think about their motivations. Why did those rioters in Los Angeles burn their own homes and destroy the businesses that supplied them with the jobs, goods, and services they needed to survive? Certainly it was more than those objectionable verdicts.

The seething rage that was unleashed those three fateful days attested to the fact that something much deeper was working in the hearts and minds of African American Angelinos. Almost thirty years had passed since the Civil Rights Act of 1964 had outlawed discrimination, and California was one of the most progressive states in terms of civil rights legislation. In legal terms, equality had been established, and its practical effects were felt even in the more remote parts of the United States.

Certainly the blacks in Tulsa in 1921 enjoyed none of the practical freedoms of the African Americans living in the early 1990s. In fact, Jim Crow laws were in full effect during the 1920s, with rampant prejudice and discrimination unchecked among whites of the same era. Yet, these blacks remained civil and only picked up arms to defend themselves from a violent mob of whites bent on destroying their homes and families. Furthermore, the blacks living in Tulsa prior to the 1921 riot were actually prospering so much that the Greenwood district was nicknamed the "Black Wall Street."

So here is the key to what changed: *Somewhere between the seventy years of these two race riots, black energy to mainstream turned into a quest for equal rights.* The blacks in Tulsa were fighting to defend their families and to protect what rightfully belonged to them. The blacks in Los Angeles were doing something entirely different—they were murdering, looting, and pillaging, all in the name of "equality."

THE NAACP: NEGATING THE ADVANCEMENT OF AMERICA'S COLORED PEOPLE

I often debate radical leftists who make the incredible claim that the United States is almost a third-world country as they cite statistics about our nation's poor. This is simply laughable, but these people genuinely believe in what they are saying. Every day on CNN we hear the progressive liberal mantra of "Equality, Equality, Equality" drummed into our heads. And the sad part is that most of us willingly accept it as the social gospel. Really, how could anyone be opposed to equality?

So what are we trying to accomplish under the mantra of equal rights? Perhaps the mission statement of the oldest and largest civil rights organization in the country, the NAACP, will give us some insight:

The mission of the National Association for the Advancement of Colored People is to ensure the

political, educational, social, and economic equality
of rights of all persons and to eliminate racial hatred
and racial discrimination.

The leader of the NAACP, Chairman Julian Bond, explained this
mission statement at the organization's 96th annual convention
in 2005, saying, "Our mission has not changed . . . We are a
social-justice advocacy organization dedicated to ending racial
discrimination. That's what we do."

Bond's explanation left me quite sad. Black America has real
problems, and the NAACP and its leaders either don't care about
them or are so out of touch with reality that they are incapable
of honestly seeing these problems. As result, the challenges facing blacks are far greater than they might otherwise be.

The truth that black leaders like Bond can't seem to come
to terms with is that the deep problems in America's black community today are not the result of racial discrimination, and
blacks do not need an organization with a $40 million budget
dedicated to "social justice."

Racism does not cause an AIDS epidemic, family breakdown, 50 percent high-school dropout rates, widespread out-
of-wedlock births, or the destruction of millions of unborn
black babies. These are real problems. But instead of searching
out real answers, America's black leaders would rather stand on
a platform yelling "Racism!" According to Bond, "Racial discrimination is a prime reason why the gaps between black and
white chances remain so wide. And we believe that to the degree
we are able to reduce discrimination and close these race-caused
gaps, we will see the lives of our people improve and their pros-

perity increase." If Bond and other leaders continue to pass the buck and avoid confronting the truth about black society, real problems will not be solved and black life in America will go from bad to worse.

Is America free of racism? Of course not. Is racism the reason why blacks lag economically in America? Of course not. The single most important factor in establishing economic earning power is education, and the single most important factor that drives the educational accomplishment of a child is family. Blacks lag economically because we lag educationally, and we lag educationally because the black family in America's cities barely exists. The weights holding down the future of black children today are problems in our own community. The fact that mainstream black leaders are incapable of being honest about these problems encourages members of our culture to remain "victims."

AN HONEST LOOK IN THE MIRROR

In the 1950s, men and women standing up for their right to be a citizen, not a victim, in society gave their lives in the hope of a better future for their people. What would they say about the progress we have made?

Even though the civil rights acts and subsequent legislation of the twentieth century brought legalized discrimination to a halt and racism on a broad scale ceased to exist, many blacks have followed the plantation ideology, continually crying "racism" as though they were being forced to pick cotton for the "massah." Some well-meaning whites in Middle America exacerbate the situation by commiserating with the black community. By advocating programs that perpetuate African Americans' dependence, they do not help; they enable.

The problems of African American society can not be solved in one or two paragraphs. But I do know that any hope for positive, lasting change requires a willingness to take an honest look at ourselves in the mirror and then make some hard choices. An individual or group cannot claim victim status for an extended amount of time without good reason for doing so. We must be honest about where we are, where we've been, and where we're going.

If we are truly honest, we as a community will find that the main problems facing black Americans aren't issues of equality. Equality is determined only by God and will come in His fashion. Rather, like the rest of American society, our main problems deal with *morality*—how are we going to act and react when faced with the various difficulties in life? Decisions with proper regard for morality, and not equality, are what are required to secure a bright future for all of America's citizens.

THE FORGOTTEN VICTIMS

With the crowd of pseudo-victims seeking the limelight on America's social stage, society's true victims are often relegated to the shadows. No parades march for the children of broken (or never established) homes; no honor ribbons exist for the elderly. Not much political capital to be made from the masses of self-created victims, either—the rising numbers of people addicted to methamphetamines, other drugs, and pornography. Nor have

I seen an official protest over the modern American-made category of victim—those injured or killed by youths who have guns but no conscience.

But of all the ignored casualties of America's *morality war*, the most tragic victims are also the most helpless, the ones with no voice to cry out in protest. In the thirty-two years since *Roe v. Wade* rocked our nation, the sterile slaughter of over forty-five million potential American lives is, for many citizens, tantamount to premeditated murder. The issue of abortion divides Americans like few others. Although the public outcry over abortion has waned a bit in recent years, convictions remain strong. No other debate hits so close to home, encompassing matters of conscience, convenience, and community.

THE UGLY TRUTH

A plethora of pamphlets and bumper stickers stand ready to argue both sides of the abortion issue. And yet, with all the ballyhooing out there, the cold, raw facts regarding abortion often get forgotten. If Americans are honest, many on both sides of the debate would rather be kept in the dark.

The numbers . . .

- In 1973, the year *Roe v. Wade* legalized abortions in our country, the Alan Guttmacher Institute (AGI, Planned Parenthood's special research affiliate) reported that about 744,600 abortions were performed. The number topped 1,000,000 two years later, reaching an all-time high (and moral low) of 1,608,600 abortions in 1990. Though the number has steadily decreased since then, it brings small comfort that in the year 2004, an estimated 1,293,000 American fetuses were aborted.

- Using current AGI figures and estimates, *the total number of abortions performed in the U.S. since 1973 equals 45,951,133.*

- The former Soviet Republic wins the dubious distinction of having the highest estimated number of total abortions in history (over 304 million from 1957 until its dissolution), but the Land of the Free ranks fourth in accumulated abortions behind China and Japan. Unfortunately, in the top five rankings of annual abortions, we take the silver medal. (With the exception of the United States, none of the societies of this morbid league of nations seem particularly "liberated.")

1. China		6,340,000
2. United States		1,293,000
3. Vietnam		1,000,000
4. India		723,000
5. Ukraine		434,000

Rounding out the top ten are Japan, South Korea, Romania, the United Kingdom, and France.

- It is hard to grasp the magnitude of the approximate 12,250,000 abortions happening in our world every year. One thing is for certain, though, in the years from 1920-2005, nearly 1 billion (945,000,000) of the world's potential inhabitants never had the chance to grasp anything.

The women . . .

Statistics for the year 2000, according to the Center of Disease Control and Prevention*:

- In 2000, 21 out of every 1,000 women aged 15-44 had an abortion, making the abortion ratio 245 per 1,000 live births.

- Of the women choosing abortions, 33% were aged 20-24, 18% were teenagers between the ages of 15 and 19, and almost 5,000 teenagers under the age of 15 had abortions.

- Of the women having abortions, 54.8% were white; 35.1% were black. Urban centers reported higher numbers of black women. (In NYC, 94,466 black women had abortions, nearly half the city's yearly total.)

- The abortion ratio for unmarried women was 8.8 times the ratio for married women.

---

*These numbers are typical of recent years. CDC researchers admit they may undercount the numbers because of the discrepancy in state laws regarding reporting abortions.

- Of the aborting women, 39.1% had never delivered a "live birth" before. (Percentages dropped sharply for each delivered child, with moms of four children making up only 4.2% of the abortion population.)

- Although the overwhelming majority of abortions are done in the first trimester, the CDC estimates that *9108 were done in the 21st week or later.*

- Out of 589,653 women choosing abortion, 25% had already had one, 10% had aborted twice, and *43,759 admitted to having already had 3 or more abortions.*

Such stark statistics rarely penetrate the modern Middle American psyche. Detached, we can even ignore that we began as the very "tissue" compiling these somber tallies. While we decide whether or not we want to fight for the rights of the unborn, the number of extinguished lives continues to rise.

EVERY CHILD A "WANTED" CHILD?

One of the main groups holding the megaphone for the proabortion crowd is the Planned Parenthood Foundation of America (PP). The other day I was surfing the Internet and stopped by their site. At the end of an article about Plan B emergency contraception, a self-absorbed and self-congratulatory paragraph announced that:

Planned Parenthood Federation of America is the nation's leading sexual and reproductive health care advocate and provider. *We believe that everyone has the right to choose when or whether to have a child, and that every child should be wanted and loved.* Planned Parenthood affiliates operate more than 850 health centers nationwide, providing medical services and sexuality education for millions of women, men, and teenagers each year. We also work with allies worldwide to ensure that all women and men have the right and the means to meet their *sexual and reproductive health care needs.* [emphasis mine]

What outright nonsense! An entire book could be written explaining the ill-conceived rhetoric stated by Planned Parenthood officials. Right off the bat, the question begs to be asked, "What are sexual health care needs?!?" In fact, the passage sounds a lot like a commercial from Home Depot . . . *Helping You with All Your Sexual Health Care Needs*: "Condoms are on aisle nine." "Could I get a price check on diaphragms?" "Abortions are two-for-one every Tuesday and Thursday!" You would think you were visiting their site to buy a roll of duct tape and some light bulbs.

But what really struck me was the sentence, "We believe that everyone has the right to choose when or whether to have a child, and that every child should be wanted and loved." We've all read similar sentiments on bumper stickers and T-shirts from the National Organization for Women (NOW) or Planned Parenthood: "Keep Your Laws Off My Body" or "Pro-Choice Pro-Child/Every Child a Wanted Child." (By the way, if you want a brief escape from rationality, visit the NOW merchandise

Web page—it might make you realize just how conservative you really are.) I had often thought about the words "every child a wanted child." Each time I saw them plastered on the back of someone's car, I knew something was desperately wrong with that statement, but I couldn't put my finger on it. After all, no one can disagree that every child should be wanted and loved. It took some serious thinking to uncover the subtle deception being propagated on the bumpers of thousands of vehicles.

Yes, every child should be a loved and wanted child. But shouldn't that love and want come from the mere fact that it is a child? Shouldn't the child warrant love and affection for the sole reason that he or she is a human baby in desperate need of care?

Not according to Planned Parenthood. To them, love and care are solely the prerogatives of the mother, and perhaps an (in)significant other. If she chooses (pro-choice) to love the unborn child, then *she* has given the baby its worth. After making the choice to love, the female breeder (mother) will carry the baby to term, providing him or her with the nutrients, clothing, and protection that she deems is necessary. It has nothing to do with any intrinsic natural rights of the child whether or not the *baby* will live. Rather, it is based upon some self-centered emotional response of the mother that determines the child's worthiness to gain membership into the human race. In the words of Tina Turner, "What's love got to do with it?"

Think about the negative alternative to the phrase *every child a wanted and loved child*: if the mother hates the child, she aborts him. Then why doesn't the National Organization for Women have a bumper sticker that says "Every Fetus an Unwanted and Hated Fetus"? I guess that doesn't really show the public their warm and snuggly motherly side. And of course they wouldn't want to use the word *child* here because the fetus only gains the status of "child" when the mother decides that she "loves" him and wants to keep him. For all their pious pandering, they are actually quite selfish. They want us to believe that what they are doing is, in the words of Hillary Clinton, "for the children," when it is actually for themselves.

The kind of love Planned Parenthood describes isn't love at all. Rather, it is just a desire by these women to live life as they wish. Meanwhile, they still manage to fulfill their narcissism by having a couple of children that they *want*. Kind of like buying a pet. First, you have to shop around for what you want. Big dog or little dog? Red dog or blue dog? Guard dog or family dog? Finally, you make the *choice* on what you *want*, and you bring little Ashton—I mean Fifi—home.

Even the word *want* has interesting connotations. *Webster's Dictionary* defines it as "to have or feel need." Certainly, women everywhere, religious or not, conservative or liberal, feel a biological need to have children. Basic studies on human nature confirm this. Something in us women craves to have children of our own, and then wants to care for them. However, radical feminists who defend the pro-abortion worldview by stating "every child a wanted child" wouldn't be caught dead proclaiming that they *want* (have a need) to procreate! Imagine the likes of Gloria Steinem stating that her motherly instinct is calling her to bring children into the world and change their dirty diapers at three in the morning. No, the kind of "want" Planned Parenthood, NARAL, and NOW mean is more akin to the want that teenage girls have when they shop at The Limited. Except they advocate returning your "purchase" before you even bring it home.

But don't just take my word for it. Listen to the words of Gianna Jessen, in her 1996 testimony before the Constitution Subcommittee of the House Judiciary Committee. Gianna is a survivor of abortion.

> Today, a baby is a baby when convenient. It is tissue or otherwise when the time is not right. A baby is a baby when miscarriage takes place at two, three, four months. A baby is called a tissue or clumps of cells when an abortion takes place at two, three, four months. Why is that? I see no difference.

THE CONSEQUENCES OF FREE CHOICE

If you take the time to dissect the messages behind powerful organizations like Planned Parenthood or NOW, you may find their reasoning highly suspect, not to mention their values or their motives. But in today's fast-paced world, few Americans ever digest more than sound-bites and headlines. For example, how many have noticed the media's shrewd labeling of the two sides of the abortion debate? People who believe in life are rarely, if ever, called *pro-life*. Instead, they are negatively described as *anti*-abortionists. On the other side, those who are in favor of chopping up and sucking out babies from the warmth of their mothers' wombs are not called anti-life. They are given the much friendlier, all-American title of *pro-choice*.

Sometimes the media flat out refuses to show another side. When *The New York Times* and *USA Today* rejected a Focus on the Family ad criticizing the U.S. Supreme Court's decision permitting the procedure known as partial-birth abortion, syndicated columnist George Will had this to say:

> If that moving but mild ad is objectionable to *USA Today* and the *Times*, then they probably consider any criticism of partial-birth abortion unfit for public consumption. Such censorship—in the name of compassion: protecting the public's tender sensibilities—represents a novel understanding of the duties of journalistic institutions.

Referring to the media's failure to report on a nurse's moving testimony (in which she tells about holding and rocking a twenty-one-week-old aborted baby with Down's syndrome for forty-five minutes rather than letting the "suffering child d[ie] alone in a soiled utility room") on behalf of a proposed Born-Alive Infants Protection Act before Congress, he said:

> Such public testimony, as well as the existence of [Florida Senator] Canady's bill, has gone almost entirely unreported. Perhaps the media, practicing compassionate liberalism, are protecting the public from the distress that would be occasioned by confronting some consequences of public policy.

This crafty handling of the debate is one reason the surface message of abortion rights activists strikes a chord even with some Americans who would never dream of having an abortion themselves. In the absence of the true, horrific facts, many choose what they see as the freedom-loving side. After all, who wants to side with the negative, angry "anti" people when you can hang with folks who are all about giving *choices* and protecting *rights?* Abortionists have used Americans' love for freedom and independence to advance their own cause.

But a society that chooses *freedom* over *values* suffers the consequences. The test of time always reveals whether stepping away from morality for freedom's sake truly makes us free. We learned that lesson with slavery. Our country still suffers repercussions from our forefathers' acceptance of that evil institute. Thank goodness, some brave decent citizens of both races finally stood up and condemned it. By choosing morality over the freedom to own slaves, our nation became a greater and freer people.

Just as it did with slavery, the social acceptance of abortion has pushed the moral envelope too far. And we are paying for it. (Not just with tax money, either.) Millions of Americans—both men and women—carry buried emotional scars from past abortions. Women's rights groups, so eager to discuss all the ways they are supporting the female sex, become strangely mute when the topic of Post-Abortion Syndrome is raised.

Far and away the worst toll abortion has taken on society has been on the most vulnerable demographic, the African American community, where black women are three times more likely to have an abortion than their white counterparts.

Thirteen million unborn black babies have been destroyed since the *Roe v. Wade* decision in 1973. How many of those babies might have grown up to be leaders and fathers in a community already diminished through crime, disease, and incarceration?

Since American black reality is a sample of American reality, the moral chaos tearing apart our community reflects a moral chaos that exists in the nation as a whole. Again, abortion survivor Gianna Jessen sums up the moral cost our country is paying for its approval of abortion:

> There is a quote which is etched into the high ceilings of one of our state's capitol buildings. The quote says, "Whatever is morally wrong is not politically correct." Abortion is morally wrong. Our country is shedding the blood of the innocent. America is killing its future.

THE "BRIGHT SIDE" OF ABORTION??

Ever the optimists, some people choose to find positives in America's cruel abortion practice. Former Surgeon General Jocelyn Elders proudly stated that, thanks to abortion, the number of Down's syndrome cases has decreased significantly in the United States. (Though I find her joy at the news shameful, I do see fewer numbers of people with mental and physical handicaps in our society than I did as a girl.) University of Chicago Professor Stephen Levitt, author of the bestseller *Freakanomics*, claimed that abortion in the early 1980s is the reason crime rates were down in the late 90s. And just think, the ever-reactive and publicity-loving activists Jesse Jackson and Hillary Clinton had no word of outrage for those statements.

I don't know about them, but I believe that each life is precious. Some of the loveliest people I have met have had one handicap or another. And to think, these people may not have made the "cut-off" today. Our country will never know the joys we have missed from the lives that never were.

FROM A SOCIETY OF VICTIMS TO A CULTURE OF DEATH

The abortion debate, with all its claims and counterclaims, continues. What started out as a seemingly benign idea—birth control—in the 1940s, evolved into unauthorized abortions in the 1960s and legalized ones in the 1970s. It morphed itself again into infanticide with partial-birth abortions, the killing of infants well into the third trimester. And, like some horror-movie zombie whose grotesque form barely resembles its former self, the methods for birth control have spiraled down to the most recent method for late-term abortions, where "doctors" induce birth and then allow the little body to "expire" on its own outside the mother's body. Who would have believed that our civilized society would sanction such barbaric practices in the name of freedom and convenience?

Incidentally, this morphing of standards is a perfect example of one problem I have with liberalism: it continues to redefine itself and its version of "morality" on a day-to-day basis. For example, we can all agree that, at least once a child is born, named, and accepted by everyone as a citizen of our world, murdering it would be wrong, right? Not according to Peter Singer, professor of bioethics at Princeton University.

One of the most controversial authors since the 1970s, Professor Singer advocates that parents should have the right to "eliminate" (code for *kill*) unwanted children. Unbelievable as it may seem, Singer is considered by many to be the leading thinker on matters concerning social engineering and the future of Western civilization.

"But, but wait . . . !" I can hear his supporters gasping: "You didn't qualify that statement! You didn't fully explain what he means by that!" That is the key problem with the abortion community and the entire culture of death it has (ironically) birthed: They put qualifications on human life. The problem only worsens as the standards are broadened by those who set themselves up as the deciders of who lives and who doesn't. Doesn't all this weighing of human value sound vaguely reminiscent of the Nazi death camps or the killing fields of Cambodia?

Singer advocates will proclaim that what the Princeton professor meant about eliminating children was that parents could dispose of a child who is severely handicapped, and they would only have that right for up to six months after the birth of the child. So what happens when, like most liberal standards, those "rules" change, adding other acceptable conditions for elimination or extending the age limit of children being destroyed? One can only fathom the depths of human depravity. But if our society continues to follow the immoral compass of the past few decades, our worst nightmares may become reality.

And by the way, in case a few Singer disciples haven't heard, Singer has already "revised" his first time table regarding the period when a child can be killed by its parents. The age-of-eligibility has already been extended to one year.

Believe it or not, for centuries Americans understood that protecting the lives of the poor and defenseless, along with any other citizen, was tantamount to securing the freedom of future generations. Even in 1973, early abortion supporters could not have imagined that *Roe v. Wade* would not only legalize abortion, but would pave the way for stem-cell research and human cloning as well.

Opponents of these scientific advances warn against science opening another Pandora's Box of ethical issues while utilitarians bypass the "would clones be truly human" question and focus instead on the clones' scientific usefulness. They imagine a future where "fully-human" people could extract new hearts, livers, and lungs from their "non-human" clones.

But what "monsters" would be created, and what damage would be done to our individual and collective psyche? For example, one pro-cloning Web site proudly boasts that endangered and extinct animals may one day be brought back to life, that a beloved family pet could be replicated so the children could enjoy it for another twelve years. But if replacing "Fluffy" is acceptable, what is to stop grieving parents from seeking to bring back a deceased child?

YESTERDAY'S MURDER IS TOMORROW'S MERCY

Euthanasia and infanticide, along with other forms of so-called mercy killing, have been making headlines for the last several years. We've probably all heard of Dr. Kevorkian, also known as Dr. Death, who has "helped" over thirty-three terminal or severely ill people commit suicide. One report states that he assisted in the suicides of over 130 patients. Today he is serving a ten to twenty-five year prison sentence after being found guilty in 1999 of second-degree murder for complicity in assisted-suicide.

Although Kevorkian is now behind bars, what happens when popular culture and our more radical and liberal legislators catch up to the Dr. Kevorkians and Professor Singers that currently haunt the passages of our colleges and hospitals? This is not as far-fetched as you might think—the Netherlands and Belgium have both passed laws granting voluntary euthanasia, and the state of Oregon passed its Death with Dignity Act in 1997, granting citizens of Oregon the right to kill themselves under certain circumstances with a doctor's prescription.

The question is, how do we reverse our course as a nation when—and not if—we cross the threshold from "voluntary" killing to the "involuntary"? In some ways, we already have—abortion is involuntary for the victim. The unborn baby has no choice or say in the matter. The much-publicized woman named Terry Schiavo had no voice either. Her existence depended on someone else. At another's prerogative, both the unborn child and the incapacitated mother were deemed unfit for the human race.

What happens to the disabled elderly man who has no family to care for him? Does he lose his right to citizenship because he is of no utilitarian worth to society and only creates a financial burden? Given the present course we are on, the answer is a resounding "yes." Polls show that many Americans support assisted-suicide and believe that Terry Schiavo needed to be relieved of her misery.

Most citizens of Middle America shudder at Peter Singer's message of infanticide. But if parents don't protect their children against the wrong-headed interpretation of liberty promoted by Singer and other radical social engineers—that liberty includes a progressive and ever-expanding list of "freedoms"— today's children may consider Singer as antiquated and old-fashioned by the time they are grown.

Call me a prophet of doom, but with almost a third of Americans approaching fifty without a spouse or children and the mounting Medicare and Social Security crisis, how long will tomorrow's workers pay for the inconvenient, the sickly, or the retired?

Who will be tomorrow's victims?

POLITICS
IN THE
GHETTO

The cultural war in relationship to politics has seen some rather dramatic changes over the past decade. In the 1990s, we witnessed President Bill Clinton establish his legacy by getting caught with his pants down in the Oval Office and randomly lobbing a few missiles into Serbia. Democrats in Congress responded to the various investigations into the administration's indiscretions by repeatedly blaming a "vast right-wing conspiracy." On the legal front, activist judges rang in the first years of the new millennium by declaring it was lawful to sodomize, but illegal to post the Ten Commandments.

In the midst of such virtuous leadership, in 2000, America elected President George W. Bush as our new leader, reelecting him four years later along with a Republican majority in both houses of Congress—all during a so-called unstable economy and a war against terrorism in Iraq. Bush was the first president in sixteen years to win the popular majority. Even among blacks—the Democrats most loyal constituency—support to reelect Bush jumped 37 percent between the two elections. Years of cultural trench warfare had given the Christian Right a massive victory.

With the exception of the Reagan years, Republican dominance was a radical departure from most of the twentieth century. Despite intermittent Republican victories, a philosophy of progressive modernism had driven our nation's political machine for at least sixty years.

So why did Americans reject modernity and rediscover the spirit of the Magna Carta on election night in 2004?

The vote was their direct response to the onslaught of

radical liberal policies of the previous three decades. The "land of the free" now meant gay rights activists demanding complete public expression, doctors performing assisted suicide, advocates of stem-cell research denouncing the oppressive religious right, and pharmacies providing morning-after abortion pills. And to top it all off, it was now "unconstitutional" to say a prayer before a hometown high school football game.

Middle America had seen enough.

IT'S THE MORALITY, STUPID!

What was the deciding factor in keeping President Bush as a major player in our nation's cultural war?

It was not "the economy, stupid!" It was moral values. According to the Associated Press, along with the war on terrorism, morality was the number one issue voters cared about in the presidential election. Bush's public and private emphasis on values resonated with America's middle class; he won overwhelmingly among the dozen swing states that chose morality as the key issue.

We can not know exactly what impact these Bush years will have on the future of American government and the Republican Party, but during his first few weeks in office, George W. began to demonstrate a moral conservatism similar to that of Ronald Reagan.

Bush's first act as president in January 2001 was to ban funding for any international groups that supported abortion. In 2003, he signed into law a ban against partial-birth abortion (later overturned by three lower courts and currently on its way up to the Supreme Court), and in his 2004 reelection bid, he called for a Federal Marriage Amendment to the U.S. Constitution that would define marriage as between one man and one woman only.

Most likely, however, the events of September 11, 2001, and the subsequent war on terror will define this president in history.

Bush's response to 9/11 was a resounding confirmation that our nation stands unequivocally for freedom and justice, and that virtues such as honor and love cannot be compromised because some left-wing activists and academic elitists insist the world is gray. In his words, 9/11 "dealt a significant blow to the philosophy of moral relativism . . . [for] it is hard to deny there is evil in the world, and that there is good."

The same majority that gave George W. a moral mandate supported his quest to bring liberty to a region long dominated by tyrants. Americans wanted safety on two fronts: from the terrorism wreaking random havoc in our modern times and from our nation's slippery slide towards Gomorrah.

The 2004 election was not merely a vote for the lesser of two evils, as some people claimed. A substantial majority of Americans had come to a consensus on morality. We agreed with Bush, that morality should be the traditional kind. We believed in the tested ideals of our forefathers and didn't want decency to die with the last member of the "Greatest Generation."

The coinciding House and Senate races confirmed convictions about George W. Bush's moral stance. Prior to the election, Republicans had 51 seats in the Senate and 227 seats in the House of Representatives. When the polls closed down, the numbers had climbed to 55 and 232. Many of these Senators and Representatives gained their seats solely over the topics of abortion and homosexual marriage.

Skeptics contend that the election of Bush and the Republican Congress was not over moral issues. (The media were thrown for a loop by the new "Values Voters." Their dropped-jawed bewilderment and collective scratching of heads were both amusing and revealing.) But how can that theory be correct when Bush openly shared his views on abortion, euthanasia, homosexual marriage, and stem-cell research throughout his campaign? In fact, besides the war in Iraq, there was little else for him to discuss. His economic agenda was well established with his first-term's implementation of the largest tax cut in recent history. Sated with low-interest rates, soaring housing values, and a $1.6 trillion dollar tax cut, Americans didn't seem to mind the roller coaster ride of his fiscal policy (or the debt it upheld).

So the only conclusion is that the people who voted for Bush chose him for his moral platform along with his stance on ter-rorism (another moral position) and homeland security. Father Richard J. Neuhaus, editor-in-chief of *First Things* magazine, outlined the self-deception of liberals who claimed "that the 'moral values' vote really doesn't mean that much":

> The argument is that the category of "moral values" is, unlike "economy/jobs" or "war in Iraq," so vague that it can mean anything or nothing. This is an argument from desperation. If nobody knew what the phrase

meant, it would seem that Bush and Kerry voters would have been more or less evenly split on "moral values." Unless, of course, one assumes that Kerry voters are in principle opposed to moral values. As it was, however, all sensate voters understood that "moral values" referred to the candidates' clear differences on abortion, embryonic stem-cell research, a marriage amendment, and, more generally, the role of morality and religion in public life. There is no other plausible explanation of the 80-18 split other than that those who named it as their number one issue thought they knew very well what is meant by "moral values."

The good news for conservatives, and for everyone else, for that matter, was that despite being dragged through Clinton's mud, a majority of Americans still hold principles that transcend the utilitarian situational ethics propagated by Tom-Hayden-wannabes. Unlike mainland Europe where marijuana is as common as french fries and homosexual "marriage" corrodes any semblance of a normal family, our nation maintains a grasp on reality. Bohemian Western Europe may have gone off the edge, but there is still hope for us.

MODERATION IN ALL THINGS?

Citizens of Middle America cannot rest on our laurels. Conservative political action groups may make a lot of noise, but as a nation we are growing more and more moderate on moral issues. How else can you explain general society's approval of unmarried cohabitation, illegitimate births, and homosexual partnerships? Why is the Bible Belt overrun with sexual diseases and small towns afflicted with drug abuse? (Experts claim that the prevalent methamphetamine abuse among the predominantly white youth in suburban and rural areas today is much worse than levels of abuse in the largely black inner-city crack epidemic of the 1980s.) Why are yesterday's vilest four-letter words the everyday lingo of today's junior high kids?

Signs of moral shifting abound, even among whites and mainline Protestants. In fact, as other ethnic and religious groups (slowly) grow more conservative—at least in their voting patterns—former bastions of conservatism move more towards the left. From 2000 to 2004, support for Bush grew among Latino Protestants, Black Protestants, and Latino Catholics. On the other hand, the Pew Forum on Religion and Public Life reported that:

> Mainline Protestants, considered a strong Republican constituency, divided their votes evenly between President George W. Bush and challenger John Kerry, producing the highest level of support for a Democratic presidential candidate in recent times from that religious group.

So what made scores of mainline Protestants cross the aisle? Unfortunately, too many have been seduced into believing an idea that has pervaded our country for at least fifty years, if not the entire century: the philosophy of materialism. The social influence of materialism today causes any public discussion to evolve into a political debate. Its contagious mindset also paved the way for America's most powerful voting block—the Moderate Middle.

The Moderate Middle is a volatile group of rich and poor, old and young, black and white, urban, suburban, and rural citizens whose political whims have been the focus of all politicians and party pollsters since the soccer moms voted for President Clinton.

For example, in 1992 Republicans declared that our nation was in a cultural war while nominee Bill Clinton concluded that only the naïve thought that values were more important than the economy. How did he know that half the nation's voters would respond to his message of materialism? A savvy liberal himself, he understood that the one consistent thread binding liberals to liberalism is selfishness.

You may question my reasoning because President Bush won the election of 2000 with half the nation's voters. True. But you did notice that in order for him to even have a shot at winning, the Republican Party had to run very far away from its social message of personal responsibility and embrace some of the big government preferences of the Moderate Middle? (The only reason that the cultural war received any attention in the election of 2004 was because aggressive homosexual activism energized a new value-voting block.)

The power of the Moderate Middle as a huge voting block is significant because they are materialists and primarily into themselves. In the same way that skewed science says, "We found a unique rock in Antarctica; there must be life on Mars," materialism says that everything that occurs in the universe, even those seemingly unexplained mysteries, is strictly the result of chemical and physical reactions. Since materialists believe that everything boils down to neutrons and electrons, they have no tolerance for those who consider the more intangibles of life. (A liberal lacking tolerance? No way!)

This intolerance was obvious in the remarks of liberal commentators following the 2004 presidential election. Outspoken *New York Times* journalist Thomas Friedman had this to say on the day after the election:

> What troubled me yesterday was my feeling that this election was tipped because of an outpouring of support for George Bush by people who don't just favor different policies—they favor a whole different kind of America. We don't just disagree on what America should be doing; we disagree on what America is.

Unfortunately for Mr. Friedman, he is exactly right. We want what America was intended to be—a nation that protects life and doesn't shirk back from defending the poor and helpless. We want an America that doesn't promote a nihilistic narcissism of perverted sexual behavior or corrupt our schoolchildren through propaganda. In other words, we want an America that encourages her people to aspire to their highest calling, one that transcends the bonds of a materialism that sees life as nothing more than the result of a primordial soup.

Thomas Frank, in his controversial book *What's the Matter with Kansas? How Conservatives Won the Heart of America,* apparently considers what happened in the election a "moral" travesty. Not so much because Bush won, but because, like Friedman, Frank can't comprehend how America's heartland could be so "deranged" as to put him in office. A critic of the book, James Neuchterlein, explained that Frank could not fathom how the now infamous red states could place moral issues over economic ones. According to Neuchterlein, Frank thinks that the masses are basically stupid, and that leaders of corporate America are malignant elements who use evil capitalism to siphon off billions of dollars from unsuspecting working-class Americans. Frank is baffled that those Americans living in the red states would vote for a party whose economic policies work against the best interests of the very farmers, grocery store managers, and engineers who put Bush into office. Obviously Frank could not conceive that Americans living in states like Ohio, Indiana, and Oklahoma might understand something he doesn't: moral issues take precedence over economic ones.

Frank wasn't the only member of culture's elite who didn't get it. I was one of the roundtable commentators for the BBC (the only news source in most of Europe, Asia, the Middle East, and Africa) on election night and the idea of blue-collar workers in Ohio voting for their moral beliefs baffled the other panelists. I was the only one on the panel insisting that this election would not be about economic interests, but about the moral future of America.

My prediction came true when, after decades of encroachment by an amoral movement demanding its "right" to do whatever-it-wants, whenever-and-wherever-it-wants-to under the imagined protection of free speech, right to privacy, or other liberal distortions of the Constitution, Americans finally said "no." Liberals are still recovering from the shock of that unfamiliar word.

THE PARTY OF GRUMPY OLD MEN

After liberals recovered from their period of mourning (and what a star-studded pity party that must have been—just imagine . . . Michael Moore, Barbra Streisand, Tim Robbins, Maureen Dowd, and Bruce Springsteen sharing the same tissue box!), they stepped up their familiar rhetoric to make sure the average American would know who the bad guys in Washington really were.

Juxtapose your mental image of progressive liberals with classic conservatives for a minute. I imagine the liberal crowd looks a bit more . . . fun (and certainly more famous). The media, along with those in academia and radical-left politicians, have painted a very ugly picture of conservatives over the years, making them out to be a club of crusty, old, rich, white, Republican men with bad tempers and a sadistic desire to control everyone in their sight. An entourage of liberals have put conservatives on the defensive, forcing them to apologize for everything they do or stand for, from supporting the military and defending marriage to praying in Jesus' name. The strategic marketing of liberal views (remember how the media dubbed pro-lifers as *anti-abortionists*?) has been successful enough to blind Middle America from seeing conservatism for what it really is.

Because of the distorted portrayal of conservatism, many Americans can not see that the ultimate goal of conservatism is freedom in its truest sense. Rather than a static object that rusts with time, American conservatism is dynamic wisdom. It affirms the dignity of humanity by reminding us that we are part of a larger story, and our role in that story is important regardless of our social position.

This recognition of our role in the great story of humankind implies that there must be a Storyteller, a Someone who at the very minimum, narrates the story of which we are a part. This is one reason that conservatives are so often today linked with religious beliefs.

The greatest task of America's conservative leaders is to continue to stand in the face of demagoguery, propaganda, slander, and filibusters and keep stating the truth. Giving in for the sake of a few more votes only encourages the enemies of liberty and justice. In this moral struggle, there is no room for compromise.

WHEN POLITICS ARE SKIN DEEP

As a black conservative, I deal with false generalizations all the time. (*Black* and *conservative* aren't often paired together.) For example, my organization once sent out a press release saying that reforming Social Security with personal retirement accounts would be good for blacks. I received a one-sentence e-mail from the editor of a black newspaper calling me an Uncle Tom.

Clearly, facts and analysis were of no interest to those who sent such mail. They had no questions about why I had drawn my conclusions. It was simply clear that if I hold a particular view, I must be a turncoat to my race. This is the case in general in black politics. It is generally assumed in the African American community that a black Republican is successful because he or she has sold out to the establishment. Again, truth is not important. Only the image that falls in line with a liberal worldview.

Doesn't anyone wonder why the NAACP has not hosted events honoring the first black woman secretary of state? Or why an organization dedicated to advancing the lot of blacks does not celebrate our black Supreme Court justice, Clarence Thomas? The issue, of course, is politics and not substance. Their goal is not a thoughtful and just world, but a world that reflects the preconceived notions of those in exercise power.

I understand the violent and sordid past that defines African American history presents a particular challenge for black conservatives. After all, the U.S. Constitution, whose original intent conservatives want to recapture and preserve, originally intended for blacks to be property. So is an appreciation of conservatism and the founding fathers unnatural and perhaps even impossible for blacks? Are black conservatives really, as black liberals say, simply sellouts to "The Man," the white establishment?

Quite the contrary. Conservatism, both black and white, conserves the timeless moral truths and ideals rooted in our nation. History did not end in 1776 or in 1789, but rather, for Americans, including black Americans, these were starting points. Without a doubt, the forced enslavement of black men, women, and children left a shameful stain on our nation's history. But the evil that upheld slavery was ultimately crushed by a greater good. Yes, it took forty-one years to convict ex-Klansman Edgar Ray Killen for the murder of three young civil rights workers in Mississippi. But justice was done. Furthermore, two of the three freedom fighters who were murdered in Alabama were white, as were thousands of abolitionists during the Civil War. These people understood that the ideals for which they fought, and for which many gave their lives, are timeless and true for people of every race, background, and history.

Recently I had a chat with one of my new neighbors. Being on the opposite side of the political and cultural fence than I, she was quite surprised to hear some of the names in my circle of friends. How could I, a black woman, associate with such right-wing conservatives, she demanded? My politics, my associates, and my view of life didn't jibe with her view of blacks as independent thinkers.

So what does this African American woman have in common with Rush Limbaugh, Chuck Colson, and millions of other white conservatives? Something unique in this age: an appreciation for how eternal truths relate to every aspect of our lives, including the role of law, politics, and government. It takes intentional effort to turn off all the noise that has flooded the airwaves of our minds and refute our own defensive arguments that avoid the truth. But once we do, Truth has room to fill the vacuum, changing our souls' very substance. When that finally happens, we begin to look for others who have the same understanding. That shared appreciation for Truth is why it is so easy for a black woman like me to identify with conservative "white folk" like Kay Hymowitz or Christina Hoff Sommers instead of liberal "black folk" like Oprah Winfrey or Julianne Malveaux.

A MODERN TWIST ON SLAVERY

If Howard Dean, Julian Bond, and other guardians of liberalism were paying attention, they would note the reaction that Bill Cosby receives on his nationwide inner-city tour. Inner-city moms and dads wait in line for hours to hear his message. After years of Democratic spin, his call to responsibility almost sounds like relief. Cosby tells parents that positive change starts by looking in the mirror, not to Washington. Cosby wants blacks to believe in themselves. Liberals wants blacks to believe in government.

Bill Cosby may be no friend to conservatives. But he does not stand for ignorance either. Cosby had some choice words for black America's parents in a 2004 speech for the National Association for the Advancement of Colored People (NAACP). After receiving criticism for airing the "dirty laundry" of the black community, Cosby replied, "Everybody can already see your dirty laundry . . . it gets out of school at 2:45 everyday and terrorizes its community."

Such blunt self-assessment in the black community is rare. After decades of liberal propaganda, most of poor America believes that they are owed something, someone else is the reason for their problems, and the federal government had better rescue them soon. Any call for personal change borders on treason. This entrenched mindset robs urban citizens of their potential, their dignity, and their freedom. As the primary laboratory for social experiments, inner-city America spreads its disease of dependence to each generation, with the pathologies of the welfare state as its most obvious symptoms.

You can trace the origins of the modern welfare system to a period in our country when morals took a nosedive. In the 1970s, the feminist movement and the sexual revolution geared up to full-throttle. Under materialism's influence, Americans had learned for decades that men and women are simply the products of evolution with no real differences between us. Women left their husbands in hopes of "reinventing" themselves, men abandoned their wives to have sex parties, and the result of all this sexual partying was inevitable: illegitimate children and devastated homes. Meanwhile, in this "God is dead" atmosphere, drug use skyrocketed, yielding a new class of addicts. In a misguided attempt to protect the children of this "free" generation, Uncle Sam stepped up with government safety nets. Its efforts decimated the already struggling black family.

Lyndon Johnson adhered to the prevailing political and social theories when he constructed his policies on welfare. Faced with a culture of dissipation, experts ignored the role individuals' destructive behavior played in the chaos and blamed The System. The resulting policies initiated millions of single mothers into the welfare mentality. Generations would be born and raised on what I call Uncle Sam's Plantation.

For the following decades, blacks have heard nothing from their leaders except that an unjust and racist America is the root of their problems, and that political action and government spending programs are their only hope. As a result of this engrained message, the growth of what is fast becoming a permanent black underclass continues, devoid of the very attitudes and values critical for people of any background or color to make it in this world.

American society's materialist worldview has nourished the welfare system. Liberal politics of envy and class struggle preach that poverty exists in our country because of the rich, and welfare is necessary and should be increased. According to John Edwards, running mate of John Kerry in the last election, "America is divided into two classes, one rich and one poor." (Did he forget that he and Kerry belong to the "evil" upper class?) Throughout the 2004 campaign, Edwards tried his best to divide the country with sound bites:

> Two Americas . . . one privileged, the other burdened . . . one America that does the work, another that reaps the reward. One America that pays the taxes, another America that gets the tax breaks.

Of course, upward mobility is completely impossible in the United States. Our "slaves" and "peasants" are bound to the same caste system as the people of India. No one here has ever worked hard to become multi-millionaires; the rich have inherited everything they have. Yeah, right. Perhaps the lure of socialism just has a better ring to it than hard work.

The Wall Street Journal and *The New York Times* recently featured stories about class and mobility in the United States. Despite drawing on largely different research, both features reached the same the conclusion: overall class mobility has been coming to a screeching halt, and not just in our overtly welfare communities.

According to the *Journal*, ". . . Americans are no more or less likely to rise above, or fall below, their parents' economic class than they were 35 years ago."

The *Times* quoted similar data, pointing out that the gap between the rich and poor is increasing. From 1979 to 2001, the after-tax income of the top 1 percent of American households increased 139 percent, the middle fifth by 17 percent, and the poorest fifth by 9 percent. While parents' economic status once contributed by a factor of about 20 percent to a child's economic destination, that range has increased to about 50 percent. It seems that in today's America, the rewards for being born into the right circumstances and the penalties for being born into the wrong circumstances are steadily growing.

The operative questions in these studies challenge conventional American wisdom and the belief in a free market: *Over time, doesn't a genuinely free, capitalist society actually become increasingly less free and fair? Won't those born into the right circumstances, meaning the right parents or the right genes, evolve to the top and the others not stand a chance?*

Certainly liberals would answer yes. Undoubtedly these studies have found their way into the hands of those in Washington who'll want to fix the "mobility problem" with legislation to level the playing field. Mark my words that class mobility becomes a 2008 election mantra.

If and when this happens, we will need to remind our politicians to keep recent history in perspective. They must recognize that the period of time that class mobility in the United States has become increasingly sluggish has also been a time of unprecedented social legislation. In the last half-century, we have waged a war on poverty, passed affirmative action, and continued to raise minimum wage. Yet in the midst of all this government assistance, income gaps have grown, and the class a person is born into has become an even more reliable predictor of the class in which he will die. The standard of living exposed during the aftermath of Katrina showed the world the real-life results of liberal social policies. A culture bred on dependence can not thrive.

Journalists are blind to evidence that some oh-so-popular American social policies have done more harm than good. Even (or especially?) prestigious news sources like *The Wall Street Journal*. The *Journal* accurately reported that "17 percent of whites born to the bottom 10 percent of families ranked by income remained there as adults, but 42 percent of blacks did," concluding that the class-mobility picture is even worse for blacks. But the *Journal* reporter's following conclusion reveals the bias that has driven racial politics for the last half-century: "Perhaps as a consequence, public-opinion surveys find African Americans more likely to favor government redistribution programs."

The reporter totally ignored that the converse of the theory might be true: *Because* blacks are more likely to favor government programs, they increase the likelihood that they will do no better than their parents. After all, generational poverty is also true for whites who favor government programs.

I would state it this way: Despite what *Forbes* and *Fortune* magazine tell you, no one can devise an exact formula for getting rich. However, we can devise a formula for getting and staying poor: Don't work. Convince yourself that your life reflects the decisions of others and not your own. Be the perennial victim. This is the chief toll that the welfare system has taken on blacks. It established a culture of poverty.

The advantage of being born into a good family is not news. If only reporters at the *Times* and the *Journal* had the courage to dig beneath political agendas and bureaucracy to ask the harder, unpopular questions about poverty in our country. What about investigating how the decline in family values affects the poor? How do children before marriage affect poverty?

The African American community has been particularly hurt by leaders who continue to promote a culture of welfare and entitlement despite the facts. Here is the truth:

- Freedom and capitalism do not reduce mobility. Mobility is lost when personal responsibility is bypassed on the road to success.

- Most Americans, regardless of race, trace their lineage to someone who was poor.

- Being poor is not a predictor of an affinity for government programs.

- Absolute dependence on government programs is a good way to remain poor, as is having and raising children outside marriage.

THE MINORITY OF TRUTH

The welfare-state culture in modern America goes well beyond the black community. Sadly, the Moderate Middle is no more engaged in the war on poverty than it is in the cultural war for morality. While generations continue to grow up with a heritage of entitlement, the Moderate Middle "contributes" by throwing billions of tax dollars at the poor, all the while hoping that these "victims" will not move on their street or attend their child's public school.

A Middle American who disagrees with welfare policies had better keep his or her mouth shut or risk becoming a political leper. Criticizing the welfare system does not play well in the press, especially if you are wealthy and white. A black mother of six subsisting on food stamps in the projects saying, "I just don't see how we're going to make it" plays better than a white woman in an SUV saying, "I just don't see how continuously giving people money for doing nothing is really good for them." Much better to show the poverty of generations of Americans and blame "the establishment" than ask tough questions about what is keeping them there.

Some are unafraid to speak the unpopular truth. One of the more sweeping articulations of the welfare system was penned in 1991 when Pope John Paul II issued an encyclical called *Centesimus Annus*. A fascinating discussion about socialism, capitalism, the welfare state and the nature of free society, the work is a deeply thoughtful and courageous document that every American, of every religious persuasion (including Evangelicals) should consider reading.

The encyclical explores the major issues of individual freedom and the role of government that we as Americans struggle with every day. Rather than calling it immoral not to wholly endorse government handouts, the pope sends a clear message that the abuse and misuse of politics and government is itself a moral problem. Here is what John Paul II had to say about the welfare state:

> In recent years the range of such interventions has vastly expanded to the point of creating a new type of state, the so-called "welfare state" . . . Malfunctions and defects in the social-assistance state are the result of an inadequate understanding of the task proper to the state . . . By intervening directly and depriving society of its responsibility, the social-assistance state leads to a loss of human energies and an inordinate increase of public agencies, which are dominated more by bureaucratic ways of thinking than by concern for serving their clients, and which are accompanied by an enormous increase in spending.

The welfare state is, of course, our limited version of socialism. Having grown up in Soviet-dominated Poland, the late Pope John Paul has keen observations about socialism that warrant our attention:

> Socialism considers the individual person simply as an element, a molecule within the social organism, so that the good of the individual is completely subordinated to the functioning of the socioeconomic mechanism. Socialism likewise maintains that the good of the individual can be realized without reference to his free choice, to the unique and exclusive responsibility which he exercises in the face of good and evil.

If only the helpless human "elements" being nurtured by a bene-
volent government realized that these programs are an insult. If
only third-generation recipients had courage to reject the easy
way. Bureaucracy's arrogant refusal to recognize a person's
capacity to make good or bad choices harms not only these individuals but also the entire society.

John Paul II earned the right to comment on social policies.
The Polish pope lived through the worst abuses of government
in the last century—Nazism and communism. He saw firsthand
the human suffering that resulted from government and politics
becoming religion itself, when dependent citizens become pawns
for government agendas. The pope aptly described the tension
of a modern citizen who lives in a socialism-leaning welfare state:

> The individual today is often suffocated between two
> poles represented by the state and the marketplace.
> At times it seems as though he exists only as a pro-
> ducer and consumer of goods, or as an object of state
> administration.

The *Centesimus Annus* ends by discussing the problems that
arise in societies that trust materialism and the government
instead of appreciating the value of life, a unique value independent of the state and market.

The Holy Father is not the first to believe that the welfare
state cripples its citizens' potential and motivation to succeed.
Nor is he the first father to preach that individual responsibility
is critical to the moral base of a nation. America's early fathers
said it too.

Along with morality, the first European settlers on our shores encouraged economic freedom and progress through capitalism and a strong work ethic. Captain John Smith is often credited with saving Jamestown by requiring the noblemen of the colony to participate in manual labor and farming. His famous line, "If you don't work, you don't eat," was the incentive necessary to encourage the colonists to provide both for themselves and for the good of the colony. Within a few short years after the 1607 founding of Jamestown, the colony developed into a commercial success. Imagine the scenario if Smith had said, "If you don't work, don't worry."

Jamestown's inhabitants would not agree with Americans today who denounce the evils of capitalism. To them, laziness was the evil to be addressed. Under their work ethic, ownership of personal property was the assumed right of every American. Even the pious Puritans firmly agreed with Calvin that money in itself was good, and that liberty's right to life is firmly tied to the right to possess land and capital. If the monarchy was allowed to illegally tax a small portion of their income, it could increase that amount until the colonists were completely depleted of their resources. They would be defenseless against any attack on their communities and eventually not be able to provide for their families and posterity—their future (and ours) would no longer be secure.

HOLDING BACK THE LIBERAL TIDE

Conservatism as a philosophy understands the inseparable link between liberty and private ownership of property. After witnessing the beginnings of social engineering by Franklin D. Roosevelt, Russell Kirk wrote *The Conservative Mind* to outline what had been understood for generations of American society and politics—the basic premises of conservatism.

President Eisenhower's inauguration in 1953 bolstered a burgeoning wave of conservative thought and scholarship. William F. Buckley was one of many pioneers fighting to hold back the tide of rampant liberalism in the face of a liberal academia and government. He founded *National Review* in 1955, saying it "stands athwart history yelling 'Stop!' at a time when no one is inclined to do so, or to have much patience with those who so urge it." With his hard-hitting magazine, Buckley tried to halt the effects of a radically advancing liberalism that had made hollow promises to a naïve society—a society waiting for the leftover scraps from the dinner tables of the elitist left. The left's core problems were unmasked after the Great Society crafted by Lyndon B. Johnson left millions of Americans in moral and financial shambles. (We would never have needed welfare reform if not for Johnson's Great Socialism!)

In 1980, our nation elected Ronald Reagan and embarked on one of the most provocative decades the United States has ever witnessed. Following conservative economic doctrine as he did in California, Reagan began to cut both taxes and spending, and as a result the country experienced the longest period of uninterrupted economic growth since record-keeping began back in 1854.

In addition to bringing down the largest Communist regime in history with our allies' help, the Reagan era also exposed the oppressive philosophy of progressive liberalism and Roosevelt's

New Deal. While both Roosevelt and Reagan appealed to the best in America, a significant philosophical difference stood between the two presidents: Roosevelt turned to government to solve the problems of the people; Reagan turned to the people to solve the problems of government.

The mid-nineties proved to be a time when many elected Republicans questioned their conservative platform. Others stayed the course. Their concentrated efforts helped persuade President Bill Clinton to sign legislation for welfare reform, a tribute to the enduring Reagan legacy.

Conservatives also won a key victory on the education front. After forty years of discussions, twenty years of battles and countless defeats, the U.S. Supreme Court finally ruled in 2003 that education vouchers are not unconstitutional. For this gift of a new opportunity, thousands of poor minority children that were trapped in failing government schools can thank Milton Friedman, the father of the school-choice voucher movement.

FROM HOTEL CLEANINGS TO COMMUNIST LEANINGS

On the other side of the aisle, African Americans steeped in a worldview of victimization have remained willing pawns for opportunistic political agendas. To capitalize on their inferiority complex, far-left politicians continue to prescribe the only "medication" that will save them from racism, sexism, and all the other "isms" out there: expansion of government spending programs. By hanging the carrot of entitlements over the heads of the needy, liberal politicians compel them to comply with the ideological demands of progressive liberalism. Today's vote for the left requires that the voter be willing to accept a host of other agenda items which he would usually oppose. If you want federal entitlements for being poor, you must also support abortion, euthanasia, and homosexual marriage.

Far too many morally conservative African Americans cash in their beliefs for the few pennies federal and state governments have taken from their neighbors. If a member of the black community steps out of line and starts to lean to the right, that person is chastised until he realigns his thinking. If he continues to reject the party line, he is ostracized as an Uncle Tom. It is not easy to "rebel" and become Republican.

Although the Democratic Party effuses with rhetoric about how it has "got the back" of African American society, beneath all its policies lies a limited view of black Americans. Howard Dean, chairman of the Democratic National Committee, acted like a graduate of the Trent Lott School of Racial Sensitivity Training at the 2005 annual convention for the Congressional Black Caucus. Incredibly, he received laughs from the left-wing when he remarked that "Republicans would need the 'hotel staff' if they wanted to fill a room with blacks."

Dean's joke tells us a lot about the man. It also says a lot about the Democratic Party that chose him to lead it out of its abyss. Dean and his party are frozen in a time warp. Their sense of the social realities of our country and the challenges confronting us haven't changed since 1965, when the best job a hard working black person could get was the bell stand of a hotel.

Would someone please tell Howard Dean that some blacks today own hotels?

Obviously, Chairman Dean knows that our secretary of state is an African American woman from Alabama. I wonder if he has met the three prominent black CEOs of Fortune 500 companies, or if he and his party appreciate that the percentage of black households earning over $75,000 a year has more than quadrupled over the last forty years. Surely he is aware that over one million blacks in this country have advanced degrees. Or are these facts inconsistent with a worldview that sees blacks as the unfortunate—and politically useful—victims of a capitalist, racist American society?

Perhaps Dean didn't notice that 1.5 million blacks voted for George W. Bush in 2004—double the black vote he received in 2000. I think that's enough to fill a room. If Dean's eyes were open he'd be aware that blacks need and seek different answers than the conventional wisdom of forty years ago, when government was the answer for every social problem.

Unfortunately Howard Dean is not the only one with his eyes closed. The entire Congressional Black Caucus thought his joke about black life in America was funny and true. Rather than face the real truth, black leaders have sacrificed their children at the altar of self-interest. They have convinced themselves and their communities that until all things are equal, blacks are forever victims. Almost from birth, this struggle for equality is pounded into the psyches of African Americans.

Black people are not the only ones driven by "equal rights." The utopian ideal of equality has been the driving force of a variety of minority and "victim" groups since the political left placed it on a permanent pedestal long ago. Their use of the word evokes images in my mind of the old Soviet Socialist Republic that used systematic violence and military force to make sure that everyone was "equal." *Equality* has become a dangerous word.

Communism has wreaked more havoc on humanity than any other political philosophy in history. Forty million slaughtered by Stalin and his cronies in the name of "equality." Eighty million massacred by Mao Tse Tung of China. Communism's appeal has less to do with good will and "equality" for all, and more to do with power-hungry leaders and envy-driven followers. Even a child practices his own brand of communism, throwing a fit because "Susie's piece of pizza is bigger than mine." Our own President Ronald Reagan made his opposition to communism quite clear, stating that "The march of freedom and democracy . . . will leave Marxism-Leninism on the ash-heap of history as it has left other tyrannies which stifle the freedom and muzzle the self-expression of the people." And yet several of the liberals' themes and arguments today seem eerily familiar.

A priest friend of mine still lives in his native country, one of the several eastern European countries once under Soviet control. He warned me that many of the sayings that he hears chanted by the American far left are the same ones, word-for-word, that were employed by the Soviet leadership in his country: "Equality! Equality! Equality!"

Sure, the idea of everyone getting the same sized "slice of the pie" sounds good in theory. But nothing is that simple. Does Middle America really want to walk the dangerous road that exalts equality above all else?

THE LEFT'S PREFERRED PROGRAMS, POLICIES, AND PATSIES

Popular society has arrived at the point where perversion is applauded, laziness is promoted, and righteousness is scorned. But how? For the increasing—and tolerant—fan base of the liberal agenda, credit the dedicated members of Team Left. In addition to the previously discussed, heavy-hitting NAACP, here are some other key members in the liberal lineup.

1. OUR NATION'S "HIGHER" INSTITUTES OF LEARNING . . .

The goal of maintaining a decidedly liberal view among "victim groups" is especially obvious on college campuses. Throughout the 1990s, entire departments devoted to African American studies were set up with one purpose: to indoctrinate the minds of young black men and women into the victim mentality. Courses offered in these programs share a decidedly leftist approach to history, economics, and sociology.

On any given day in college classrooms across the United States, conservative blacks are derided as traitors, and the history of both white and black America is revised to fit the left's political agenda, regardless of how mythological its claims might be. For example, at Harvard University's Department of African and African American Studies, a description of a course entitled "Topics in African American History and Society: Changing Concepts of Blackness" says that it:

> Introduces topics in African American society and history by focusing on a general theme—changing concepts

of blackness. Using a wide range of empirical and theoretical materials, we problematize what constitutes "race" and "blackness." We explore issues of class division, regional variation, immigration, intermarriage, sexuality and gender, the social conditions which give rise to such formations, and their relation to political and cultural constructions of blackness.

What is "blackness" and how do concepts of "blackness" change unless there is a consensus about black identity to begin with? According to at least another class at Harvard, conceptions of what it is to be black are decidedly anti-conservative and anti-free market. "Marxist Theories of Racism" offers the Harvard intellectual the myopic and monolithic liberal party line of what it means to be African American:

> Marx himself doesn't say much about racism. However, many social scientists and historians have attempted to extend Marx's ideas to explain the phenomena of racial oppression and racial antagonism. We critically examine several Marxist and neo-Marxist accounts of racial ideology, the construction of racial identities, the relationship between class exploitation and racial subordination, and the role of capitalist development and expansion in creating racial inequality.

With such renowned liberals as Cornell West having served on its faculty, it's no wonder that Harvard's narrow vision of "blackness" is the only one to be found in its course catalog. The ivory tower of academics continues to follow an ideology that perpetuates the plantation mentality to ensure that dependence on the Democratic Party will continue.

(Incidentally, in this book I use the terms *black* and *white* numerous times in an attempt to explain two different worldviews that happen to correspond in a very general sense with those races. I am not seeking to define or explain the races themselves. To try to do so would be foolish, as each member of every race is a unique individual with his or her own set of circumstances. My pigment is only skin deep, so to center my or anyone else's identity around skin color only demonstrates how superficial liberal politics really are. After all, wasn't the primary goal of the civil rights movement to focus attention on character and not skin color?)

Oh, yeah . . . if "changing concepts of blackness" is not your cup of tea, don't worry. College catalogs are brimming with titillating courses. Here is just a small sampling of classes offered at some of our most prestigious schools: The Sociology of Gender; Dating and Mating: Hookup Culture at Duke; Introduction to Lesbian, Gay, Bisexual, and Transgender Studies; Pornography and Prostitution in History: Doing It, Getting It, Seeing It, Reading It, (whose discussion of sexual topics includes "distinctions between pornography and erotica").

Gives a whole new meaning to the term "liberal arts."

2. BUT I THOUGHT CORPORATE TYPES WERE REPUBLICAN . . .

Far too little attention is given to the fact that, although big corporations are institutions that supposedly promote freedom and capitalism, in reality they fight harder to promote progressive liberalism.

Today, for instance, Americans face major crises in our health care and Social Security systems, yet one would be hard-pressed to find a single corporation that is helping to advance the current administration's market-based reforms of medical savings accounts or personal Social Security accounts.

Big corporations are not only out-to-lunch regarding public policy reforms intended to reduce government and advance individual freedom and choice; they also regularly advance a left-wing agenda that increases the scope of government and undermines freedom and traditional values. Such actions are often done under the guise of helping minorities. But they result in the opposite.

A good example of big-business thinking can be seen in a *Wall Street Journal* column by Howard Paster, executive vice president of the WPP Group, one of the nation's largest advertising and public relations conglomerates. In it, he argued that a recent defeat by the House of Representatives of the Federal Marriage Amendment made both moral and business sense. According to Paster, 40 percent of Fortune 500 companies now offer health insurance to gay domestic partners. Unlike the situation with married heterosexual couples, where these benefits are received from their corporate employer tax-free, homosexual benefits must be treated as taxable income for domestic partners. As a result, corporations have an extra administrative burden to maintain one set of books for married heterosexual couples and a separate set for gay partners.

Do you see how subjective Paster is in his use of the term

"moral"? If Paster really wanted to make the healthcare market and workplace more efficient, moral, and free, his article would call for the complete elimination of the IRS provision that allows companies to provide employees untaxed health care benefits. This would open the door for more insurance plan options and allow individuals to have their own private tax-deductible health care savings accounts.

(Many of you in the Moderate Middle balk at the idea of taking the responsibility of healthcare away from the government, but health care purchase decisions belong in the hands of individual consumers. Furthermore, Christian taxpayers should not be forced to subsidize the domestic partner benefits given by corporations to homosexuals.)

The true moral dimension that Paster, other corporate executives, politicians, and the Moderate Middle should consider is the gross inequities between the current system of untaxed corporate health care benefits and the benefits for our nation's low wage workers. The *Wall Street Journal*'s Holman Jenkins reports that, as result of this system, a high-end worker gets a 40 percent discount on health insurance, and a low-end worker gets nothing. So the domestic partner of a high-end corporate staffer receives a tax subsidy for his healthcare, and the ex-welfare mother of three who answers the phones in my CURE office in Los Angeles is left to hang out to dry. This system is not only inefficient, but immoral and unfair.

Since I rarely hear the Pasters of the corporate world bring up such problems, I can only conclude that the policies that he and a good portion of corporate America now promote in the workplace—in the name of what they call tolerance and diversity—are really promoting a particular social agenda. You cannot place gay marriage and traditional marriage on the same level, suggesting they are equally legitimate lifestyles, and call that being value-neutral and "tolerant." Corporations should be honest about the major role they play in undermining traditional values when they advance a clear and explicit left-wing social agenda.

An absurd example of the left's sway over corporate America was on display—or actually, *not* on display—during the 2005 Christmas season. And did I say *Christmas?* I meant *holiday* season. After all, I don't want to injure the delicate sensitivities of any Muslims, Jews, or atheists out there!

Conservative groups launched an e-mail campaign after observing a widespread anti-*Christmas* agenda among retailers. Scroogism was now PC. Not only did companies like Target ban the beloved Salvation Army ringers from their premises, businesses were banning the term *Christmas* as well. In the myriad of Santas, holly, and other festive baubles, the actual name for the holiday was oddly absent. Of course, the stores denied any outright political reason for selling "Holiday Trees" and saying, "Have a Merry Yuletide Season," but the millions of Americans buying their merchandise didn't buy their line.

Promotion of an agenda in the corporate workplace that undermines traditional values is a negative development for the welfare of all Americans, but once again it hits our inner cities particularly hard. As conservative commentators have long argued, the collapse of the black family sits at the root of the social problems in the black community. This collapse is the product of the welfare state, brought to us by the same left-wing elitists and corporate bigwigs who are bent on the destruction of any hint of biblical morality.

3. AFFIRMING NON-ACTION . . .

Blaming others for one's disadvantages, shortcomings, or sins is the ultimate politics of control. And a community that has adopted the victim mentality is easy prey to any propaganda that seems to empathize with its situation or affirm its citizens' self-pity.

Although the Thirteenth, Fourteenth, and Fifteenth Amendments ensured the rights of blacks as American citizens, and subsequent civil rights acts reinforced those freedoms, this progress was not enough for modern civil rights activists, whose existence depends on the perpetuation of black victimization. Something else was needed to make sure that African Americans were given the necessary boost to make it in modern American society—a political remedy called affirmative action.

While affirmative action started out as an outreach initiative that encouraged employers to seek out qualified minorities, it quickly turned into a legislatively mandated program based on quotas and preferential treatment that retards the growth of black Americans in all fields of work and academics.

Rather than seeking employment and educational opportunities based on their skills and merit, a large majority of the black community turned to affirmative action as a cure-all for the "racism" they encountered. By buying into the politics of control, blacks unwittingly prevented themselves from being truly successful in their own right, without government intervention.

The lack of free-thinking black intelligentsia who reject the liberal party line about affirmative action and other policies is astounding. Such unquestioning acceptance suggests that African Americans have succumbed to a kind of mental deprivation, not because our genetic makeup is inferior as true racists would argue, but because we have closed our minds. While it is true that all men are created equal, there is a tremendous difference between equality of opportunity and equality of results. Liberal politicians have convinced Black America that it deserves both.

The Civil Rights Act of 1964 was written for the sole purpose of eliminating discrimination and making sure that every American has the same opportunity to vote, gain an education, and find work. However, just because people are availed the same opportunity to succeed doesn't mean that everyone will end up in the same place. A cursory look around our society makes this obvious—not everyone was born with Lance Armstrong's stamina or Halle Berry's looks. (I know these two have worked hard for their achievements; they just got a head start.) Individuals of every race are born with different skills and aptitudes that can lead to a wide spectrum of material success. Some people operate on brains, others on machinery. Society needs both.

The political left, however, would decry these natural inequalities as injustices in need of investigation and repair. If "Robert" and "Fred" begin at the same school, and Robert goes to college and Fred doesn't, there must be a problem. The fact that Robert didn't bother to pick up a book during school is irrelevant; he is obviously the victim of discrimination.

For progressive liberals, equality of results is the benchmark of a society free of prejudice. They honestly believe that everyone should be able to achieve relatively the same level of personal success if racism is eradicated. If large discrepancies in terms of success exist, then racism must be the reason and something must be done. Rather than being told to look inside and see if they can improve themselves, minority groups are encouraged by liberal politicians and university professors to look to government for remedies to racism.

Again, the victims of Hurricane Katrina are a perfect example of liberal policies gone amuck. Certainly, the people of urban New Orleans were the unfortunate victims of a massive natural disaster. But they were also the "victims" of something else: first, they were imprisoned by their own acceptance of a life of poverty and dependence, and second, they were victims of the social policies that promoted this self-limitation.

The consensus of African American leadership and society agrees that white liberals are right—white America is to blame for everything, from the number of young black men in jail to the number of stranded single mothers after Katrina. Can they not see the irony in believing *white* liberals who say that *whites* have lied to them and are to blame for all their societal ills?

4. INTRODUCING TODAY'S HOST OF *THE BLAME GAME:* THE REVEREND AL SHARPTON . . .

Speaking of black "leadership," I never thought I'd be nodding my head in agreement with Al Sharpton. However, I certainly was when, at the conclusion of his 2004 address to the Democratic National Convention, he noted that only in a country as great and free as ours could someone like him run for the nomination for the presidency. Unfortunately, I had to digest a litany of impassioned distortions and insults to America, its people, and African Americans in particular before Reverend Al stumbled onto something true.

Drawing on the vast foreign-affairs experience he acquired on the streets of Brooklyn, Sharpton opened his remarks by criticizing President Bush's foreign policy. (It was entertaining to hear the man who achieved fame through the Tawana Brawley charade attack the president for supposedly misleading the nation.) Clearly, Sharpton let our black secretary of state and our black national security adviser off the hook for supposedly misleading the nation on Iraq because, in his view, they—like all black Republicans—were just puppets who could not be held responsible.

Nevertheless, it was Al's moment in the spotlight, a golden opportunity to deliver a much-needed message to the thousands of African Americans in inner cities around our country. And what did the good Reverend tell them?

Something to this effect: *Government doesn't care about your personal life, your moral life, or how you conduct yourselves as citizens. We can make them pay for all this neglect and prejudice by making sure the government gives us our due—food stamps and housing.*

This is exactly what a community that is being torn apart by AIDS, illegitimacy, abortion, crime, and 50 percent school dropouts needed to hear. Particularly from someone who calls himself a minister. He might as well have been Kanye West.

Sharpton then went on to infer that without political

intervention, Clarence Thomas would never have gotten through law school. Another beautiful message to black children: *You'll never make it on your own. You're a basket case without the government. And there's no way that the black man who is a justice on the United States Supreme Court is there because of his brains and talent.*

Is it any wonder that our black community has problems? In Al Sharpton's worldview, blacks who are making it in our country today fall into two categories: those who are making it because government makes it possible for them to make it, and those who are making it because they have been bought off by the white establishment. And he is one of the most influential leaders in the African American community today. (Almost makes you miss the Reverend Jackson.)

The idea that a black man or woman has innate ability and can make it under any circumstances with faith, values, and hard work is either incomprehensible to Al Sharpton or too at odds with his career path to be given any credence.

Frankly, I would have found Sharpton's remarks much more interesting if he had chosen to answer Bill Cosby's questions about why blacks are not waking up to the fact that they need to dump the politics of impotence and victimization and start taking personal responsibility for their lives.

The fundamental problem with the politics of control preached by the Reverend Al and others is that the playing field blacks say they want leveled can never be, at least not without radical—and I mean radical—government intervention. Even then, there must always be someone at the top running the show. (It's called the *politburo,* and an excellent example of this form of government can be found in the encyclopedia under "USSR.")

A completely egalitarian society can never occur because individuals are unique, one-of-a-kind beings; each person must find his or her own way in this world. No matter how many social policies you implement, society will always contain people who are motivated to succeed, and people who are content with mediocrity. Jesus said, "The poor you will always have with you," not because they have no hope, but because there will always be those who will live a life less desirable than the one many others would want to live. Unfortunately, under the influence of the progressive liberal view of radical egalitarianism, blacks carry entrenched expectations of an impossible society. Instead of digging in their heels and putting their individual God-given talents to use, a large segment of African American society sits on the dock, waiting for their ship (or government check) to come in.

5. UNIVERSAL HEALTHCARE: IT FAILED MISERABLY IN CANADA. LET'S TRY IT HERE . . .

In 2005, I had the displeasure to learn that since the federal proposal of the previous administration failed, several state legislatures have proposed resolutions for universal healthcare within their own states. Universal or national healthcare coverage is one of the left's past and present bailiwicks. Whenever possible, they portray America's private sector as part of an evil empire of capitalism that seeks to squeeze every last dime out of the honest, working-class individual.

The incorporation of medicine into the overall plan for a "USSA" has made greater inroads than you might think. Even though the American free market has allowed for the greatest advances in medical research of anywhere in the world, many people naively believe that the former Canadian health coverage system would better meet the needs of the everyday American citizen. In fact, to many uninformed Americans, government control over health-related issues sounds like a godsend. Who wants to think about the costs of removing a tumor when all of your credit cards are maxed out?

But, rather than giving the best treatment to citizens, universal health coverage only forces them to wait in long lines, even if suffering from life-threatening conditions. This problem compelled the Supreme Court of Canada to overturn their universal healthcare system—too many people were dying from having to wait for mediocre care at best. Canadians who could afford it traveled to the United States where private doctors, unrestrained by government bureaucracy, are able to use the latest technology to save patients and substantially extend their lives. And we want to adopt a system they tried and rejected?

The worst thing about the concept of universal healthcare is that medical practitioners who have moral hesitancies about abortion, euthanasia, or stem-cell research could be excluded from practicing. Believe me, there is now a high-speed track to force all students of medicine to perform an abortion. Doctors and nurses are already criticized for clouding their professional decisions with their moral beliefs. In order to receive a license to practice medicine (remember "universal" means government-controlled), and with the way the courts have been ruling, healthcare specialists will not be able to discriminate against an individual's "right" to slap on a birth control patch or to kill their unborn child or aged parent. If you think that I sound like a conspiracy theorist, go talk to your local Christian pharmacist.

6. CELEBRATING DIVERSITY EQUALS PERVERSITY . . .

Liberals (and perhaps all politicians) are experts at manipulating language. For example, the word *diversity* is so often used that it seems to have lost any of its original meaning. The United States is a diverse society compared to others in that there are more ethnic groups residing here than in any other country in the world. However, "diversity" in the last twenty years has become liberal code for trampling upon anything that resembles traditional morality.

Just take a glance at the DiversityInc Web site and you will see for yourself. The Web site, sponsored by corporations such as ADT, Wachovia, Ford, Comcast, TimeWarner, Comerica, L'Oreal, Marriott, Pitney Bowes, Citigroup and many, many other biggies, goes to great lengths to discuss the benefits of including GLBTs in hiring. (In case you have not been enlightened, GLBTs stands for Gays, Lesbians, Bisexuals, and Transsexuals.) This is today's diversity in the workplace.

In today's public school classroom, a diverse society is one in which all cultures and their respective beliefs are celebrated— except for Christianity. Teachers earn stars for designing lessons that center around Hinduism or Islam. Rural schools take field trips to explore mosques. But if Johnny wants to bring a Bible for Show and Tell, forget it.

In Middle America, the word *diversity* allows some guilty-prone whites to absolve themselves of any culpability they feel for their great-grandfather's actions. In other words, by "celebrating" diversity, they, too, can become righteous in the eyes of those victim groups who have accused them of being white.

The liberal ideal of promoting diversity, no matter how artificial the means, has been elevated to the status of a sacred virtue. If a school chancellor or an employer promotes diversity, he is serving both the community and the national religion of radical liberalism. However, if a Christian childcare center does not want to "diversify" its teaching staff by hiring a transsexual, they are accused of being sexist homophobes even if by the law no discrimination has occurred.

7. OF MICE AND MEN, THE ENVIRONMENTAL PROTECTION AGENCY . . .

The environment is another arena in which progressive liberalism has seized an almost fascist control. While we're all familiar with the radical environmentalists who sit atop redwood trees and eat granola, most of us do not realize that a liberalized interpretation of the Constitution has created government entities with despotic powers to protect animal rights above the common interest or good.

Who would have guessed that all those serene birdwatchers and nature lovers would come together to form the perfect example of a liberal dictatorship, the Environmental Protection Agency (EPA)! In an article by The Claremont Institute entitled "Is the EPA 'The Very Definition of Tyranny'?" the authors explain how the EPA has been given carte blanche authority to establish air quality standards. True, some standards are necessary to maintain a healthy environment both for humans and animals. But what happens when these unregulated environmental entities abuse their power? Here is the Claremont Institute's answer:

> Independent administrative agencies, run by government officials who are neither elected to their new lawmaking capacity nor answerable to the chief executive, combine the lawmaking, executing, and judging functions of government in a single place—the "very definition of tyranny," according to James Madison.

In other words, these agencies, unaccountable to anyone except themselves and funded by a virtual fountain of taxpayer dollars, are able to set any standards they want.

Do you remember the big brush fires in Laguna Canyon in California? For years, the EPA wouldn't allow the owners of those public and private lands to do a controlled burn to remove dried or overgrown brush. Why? The habitat of a certain mouse species would be threatened. As a result of the EPA's fanatical policy, the brush continued to grow until it was so combustible that one spark set off a raging, uncontrollable fire. In the end, the mouse got to live a little longer before it was destroyed along with several hundred homes and seventeen thousand acres.

India has its sacred cows; America has its sacred mice.

8. THE WARM, FUZZY FEELING OF FRUITLESS DONATIONS . . .

The liberal belief that government is the answer to all social ills extends beyond our own borders. While I was writing this chapter, Scotland hosted the 2005 G8 Summit. A number of high-profile musicians staged a concert called Live 8 this same week to bring "awareness" to the financial problems facing Africa. They called on the leaders at the G8 Summit to erase the debt of those African nations that are in poverty.

Sure enough, when President Bush met with the heads of the other major industrialized nations, one major question on the table was poverty, particularly in Africa. The consensus of opinion was predictable: there is too much poverty, rich nations are not doing enough to help poor nations, and we must remedy the situation is by giving more aid.

Certainly, no one would challenge the premise that there is too much poverty in our world. Yet, why poverty exists and how to fix it are much more complicated issues than Bono and friends would have us believe.

The International Monetary Fund published a study authored by its chief economist that cast doubt on the effectiveness of aid in reducing poverty and producing economic growth. The study, which garnered a front page headline in the prestigious *Financial Times*, warned that aid can cause just the opposite.

The IMF study was not the first to question the effectiveness of foreign aid in reducing poverty. Although conclusions of previous studies vary in nuance, it is fair to say that there is no direct correlation to spending aid money and eliminating poverty.

Why is it not that simple? First, it is important to distinguish between humanitarian and development aid. Few question the importance of charity and assistance under extenuating circumstances like disaster relief. At issue is the validity of using aid as an effective tool to eliminate poverty. Second, we must consider the pure emotional appeal of aid. Who among us hasn't wanted to write a check after a heartrending commercial featuring the hungry, sad faces of children? It seems cold and heartless not to spend when poverty and suffering exist. Because the call for aid carries such a powerful emotional component, it readily lends itself to political demagoguery. To sell the idea that Americans are selfish, it is easy to juxtapose a picture of a fat American eating a cheeseburger with one of a starving African.

Another study, published by the International Policy Network in London, reported that after $400 billion in aid expenditures to Africa from 1970 to 2000, *the correlation between the aid and economic growth was negative.* Increases in aid actually resulted in worse economic performance. General explanations for this negative correlation between aid and economic performance are that aid discourages the very activities that produce economic vitality—savings, investment, and incentives for government policies that encourage and sustain positive economic activity.

I can't help thinking about how these world studies correspond with the readily available evidence about the downtrodden members of our own country. Despite decades of increased aid, our nation's poor remain more trapped in poverty's cycle than ever. Allow me to borrow a line from television's Dr. Phil when I ask proponents of increased government assistance, "How's that working for you?"

If we change the question we ask regarding poverty, the picture of the problem becomes clearer. Rather than ask how to spend money to eliminate poverty, we should examine the conditions that allow prosperity to occur.

The correlation between prosperity in nations and the conditions of economic freedom in those same nations is absolutely clear. In partnership with a network of think tanks around the world, the Fraser Institute in Vancouver, Canada, publishes an annual *Economic Freedom of the World* study, which uses measures of economic freedom along with economic and regulatory management to rank nations by their level of economic freedom.

The data clearly show that the less economically free a nation is, the more likely it will be poor. The more economically free a nation is, the more likely it will be prosperous. In particular, the 2004 *Economic Freedom of the World* study showed that the highest quintile of economically free nations have an average per capita GDP of $26,106. The nations in the lowest quintile of economic freedom have an average per capita GDP of $2,828.

The Heritage Foundation publishes a report, *The Index of Economic Freedom*, each year that reports similar results. It displays a graph showing geographic distribution of various regions according to economic freedom and income. Africa is by far disproportionately represented on the side of the graph that is economically not free and poor.

Despite these economic truths, as President Bush discussed global poverty with other world leaders, he was under great political pressure to agree to address poverty by sending aid rather than by advocating policy reforms, particularly in Africa. Europeans are forever looking for angles to blame America for the world's ills. And they are not alone. Pastors from some of the largest black churches in the United States recently wrote to the president urging large increases in U.S. aid to Africa. And you can always count on blame-happy liberals to fling the race card if "rich, white, imperialist America" hesitates to send money Africa's way.

But before we say "there, there" and addict another nation to our government's milk, we should remember three things: First, we are the most generous country on earth. Americans delivered $80 billion to the developing world in aid and assistance in 2004 alone. Of this $80 billion, over $60 billion came from private rather than government sources. Second, Americans have the capability to provide this benevolence because we are free, and freedom produces prosperity. Third, haven't we learned anything from our own nation's dependence on the government since Roosevelt's New Deal? Often we are too moved by emotion to see straight. Think about it. If you really believe our government should erase the debts of other countries to help them in their need, then "go and do likewise" and dip into your savings account so your next-door neighbor can pay off his Visa.

Citizens of Middle America must have the wisdom to seek solutions that will bring about lasting change instead of responding with knee-jerk compassion to the problem of global poverty.

THE U.S. LEGAL SYSTEM: WITH LIBERALISM AND JUSTICE FOR ALL

Another arena where the tyranny of liberalism has raised its ugly head is in a progressive justice system abounding with lawsuits. The game plan of lawyers has become so predictable that the phrase "playing the race card" is now common slang. Vague charges accusing defendants of discriminating against one group of people or another are as common as Hollywood Democrats. Former Supreme Court nominee Robert Bork explains the rash of perceived injustices in his famous book *Slouching Toward Gomorrah*:

> Structural charges [of racism or sexism] are merely silly, a way of insisting that there must be discrimination although no one can see it. Structural racism or sexism would have to manifest itself in a series of individual acts of discrimination. That equally or better qualified blacks, Hispanics, or women were denied jobs or promotions in favor of white males would be provable, and anti-discrimination laws and agencies would come into operation. Structural theories are simply an admission that actual discrimination cannot be shown, coupled with an unsupported assertion that it must nevertheless be pervasive. Only modern liberals and people with a vested interest in discovering racism would advance such an empty theory.

Easily offended plaintiffs and responsibility-avoiding defendants have joined power hungry lawyers to make a veritable carnival of our justice system today. Joining the circus are judges who have decided that creating law is no different from interpreting it. Their activism stems back to the leftist-led departure from the strict interpretation of the Constitution. Under the progressive principle that the Constitution is a "free" and "living" document that must be reinterpreted with each new generation or cultural shift, many federal and state judges have assumed the responsibility and prerogative to tilt the law towards their own worldview.

Forget the Constitution or the will of the people—these so-called justices have thrown justice out the window in favor of imposing their own myopic belief system. Placing individual rights above the public good, they use a subjective barometer to include or exclude certain behaviors as "rights." Right to sodomy? Good. Right to judge sodomy? Bad. Right to smoke marijuana? Good. Right to smoke cigarettes? Bad. Right for husband to kill Lacy Peterson? Bad. Right for husband to kill Terry Schiavo? Good.

Remember, the judiciary is not supposed to create law. Our forefathers gave this job to our federal and state legislatures, duly elected groups who represent the people. Even so, numerous judges in the last two decades have ignored this critical (and foundational) detail, wielding their power to promote their own liberal political and social agendas.

The opening of two Supreme Court justice seats brought judicial philosophy to the cultural forefront in late 2005. Like many other discussions in our country, debates about legal decisions tend to center on the differences between the "liberal" and "conservative" approach. According to political pundits, liberal judges practice "activism" and view the Constitution as a "living document" while conservatives apply "restraint" and focus on "original intent."

But society is missing the real issue. When contemplating a

potential judge's qualifications, we should ask a more funda-mental question than where the person stands on the hot-button issue of the day. Instead, we should ask: "What is the purpose of the law?"

After studying various judges' votes on several recent deci-sions regarding race, religion, and property rights, I have found these fundamental differences: a conservative views the core purpose of the law as individual protection, and a liberal sees the law's purpose as a tool for social engineering. In the con-servative approach, the law is regarded as a product of the wisdom of the ages, with the only surprises coming from how the law might apply in modern times. Liberal judges, on the other hand, see society as a social experiment where legal phi-losophy is based on whatever thinking is en vogue among the social engineers.

Take William Fletcher, for example. Nominated to the Ninth Circuit Court of Appeals by President Clinton, Fletcher believes that "the presumption of illegitimacy may be overcome when the political bodies that should ordinarily exercise such discre-tion are seriously and chronically in default." On the surface his statement appears neutral, but water does, too—when it's not being poured over your head scalding hot. Certainly judges in the 1950s applied Fletcher's philosophy in an appropriate man-ner to stop local governing bodies in the South from excluding blacks from mainstreaming. In today's liberal context, though, anything goes.

If your state legislature passes a law that does not pass muster with the personal worldview of a judge like Fletcher, he and other like-minded liberals will "correct" the situation by striking down that law. Whether their new precedents abide by society's moral codes is, in their minds, irrelevant.

A particularly egregious example of judicial activism occurred when Margaret McKeown, also on the Ninth Circuit Court of Appeals, "led the fight to disallow a Washington state ballot initiative denying special rights to homosexuals." (I guess *disallow* sounds more noble than *destroy* or *squash*). Through her office, she actually prevented a certain group of citizens from performing a civil act equivalent to that of voting.

Entering a state ballot initiative is a normal legal procedure. Many states allow their people's voice to be heard in this way. Residents in my home state of California place initiatives on the ballot all of the time. (I once spent an hour in the polling booth reading through and voting on some nine different initiatives!) I don't know all the specific guidelines required to propose an initiative, but I do know that one judge should not be allowed to stop a citizen group who has followed them. For McKeown to wield her powers in this manner usurps the authority of the Constitution and puts the liberty of the American people at serious risk. As one scholar noted,

> Now, if McKeown's opposition had been confined to lobbying against the measure so be it. That is her constitutionally protected right. But her efforts were far more sinister: She attempted to keep Washington voters from deciding on the measure at all.

Judges Fletcher and McKeown are not alone. The number of bizarre rulings dotting our newspapers in the past four decades confirms that liberal judges have moved up the ranks of the judiciary and are now practicing powerful "bench legislation" against our nation's moral well-being.

Unfortunately for Judge McKeown and her cronies, all the judicial activism on behalf of gays seems to have backfired, catapulting a rush of people to the polls in 2004 who would come to be known as "Values Voters." (One unsuspected demographic the gay support summoned was a group long nurtured by the liberal agenda, the African Americans.)

Besides bringing out angry voters, judicial activism has spawned conservative legal action groups who advocate judicial restraint. Although these organizations are a step in the right direction, what woeful rulings might have been avoided if Middle America had spoken up sooner?

THIS LAND IS MY LAND— OR SO I THOUGHT

A liberal view towards the Constitution has seated itself among those at the pinnacle of the United States legal system, the Supreme Court.

The Supreme Court's imminent domain decision in the *Kelo v. City of New London* raised eyebrows all over the country. Our forefathers wisely included the right of "imminent domain" in the Fifth Amendment because they knew that private property would at times be needed for the "public good" of building roads or hospitals, for example. What made *Kelo* a landmark Supreme Court decision is that the land seized in the case was to be used for *private* development. With the Supreme Court's 5-4 decision, the highest court in the land forced one group of citizens to give up their land so that another group could use it to make millions of dollars on, among other projects, a riverfront hotel and a health club. The "public good" of the transaction was to be the tax revenue the buildings generated!

It is mind-boggling that the *Kelo* ruling wielded the law not to protect individuals, but to evacuate them from their homes for business profit. How could the Supreme Court arrive at that conclusion? In preceding years, under the guise of approaching the Constitution as a "living and breathing document," creative judges had altered the meaning of *public use* to justify transferring property from one group of private citizens to another group whose intentions for the property appealed more to these judges. Thus activism set the stage for *Kelo*.

At least the *Kelo* decision opened the eyes of middle-class America. For decades, imminent domain interpretations had taken the property of poor, urban, and rural communities. (The Cato Institute estimates that, between 1950 and 1980, about one million families, perhaps four million individuals, were displaced from their homes by federally sponsored urban-renewal condemnations.) Along with private poor folks being forced out of their homes so suburbanites could have a faster route to the airport, middle-class folks could now lose their home for a fitness center or office complex. Liberalism's legal tentacles had reached Middle America.

THOU SHALT NOT POST THESE

On June 27, 2005, the Supreme Court dropped another bombshell against morality and legal consistency. Ruling five to four, these all-knowing justices decided to ban the display of the Ten Commandments in certain courtrooms and on certain government lands. Sandra Day O'Connor, concurring with Justice Souter, wrote:

> At a time when we see around the world the violent consequences of the assumption of religious authority by government, Americans may count themselves fortunate: Our regard for constitutional boundaries has protected us from similar travails, while allowing private religious exercise to flourish.

This would be laughable if she was not serious. Our republic's history is filled with references to religion and religious symbols, mainly the Judeo Christian kind. In our most sacred (can I use that word?) halls of government, political leaders from George Washington to George W. have referenced the divine. Visitors to Washington would find that a painting of Sacagawea being baptized hangs in the rotunda of the Capitol building, a chaplain still serves the U.S. Senate and House of Representatives, and a relief statue of the face of Moses stares directly at the Supreme Court as they make these inconsistent decisions.

Yet, despite these and more Biblical images scattered throughout historical architecture, O'Connor implied that our government assumes religious authority by having the Ten Commandments in a courtroom, and that doing so could lead to violent consequences. How can the learned men and women who sit in the highest elected or appointed offices of our great nation misinterpret such fundamental facts about the role of Christianity in our founding? How confused can we as a nation be?

(GAY) AMERICA'S MOST WANTED: THE BOY SCOUTS OF AMERICA

Speaking of confusion, who would have guessed that of all the people who have suffered the wrath of a justice system gone haywire, one of the hardest hit groups would be the Boy Scouts of America? Most of us would never harbor any ill will towards a group with its reputation for instilling the values of honor, patriotism, faith, and responsibility into our nation's young men. (Indeed, reason has taken a vacation when little boys in tents are the bane of society.) Yet left-wing and gay activists have received the sympathetic ear of activist judges in their quest to either annihilate or radically transform the Boy Scouts. Forget about tying square knots or helping old ladies across the street. The kind of scout the liberals envision is one who renounces both God and morality, openly discusses homosexual sex, and tells religion to take a hike.

Do you think I'm exaggerating?

In 2000, the United States Supreme Court decided a landmark case, *Dale v. Boy Scouts of America*. James Dale, an assistant scoutmaster, was dismissed from the BSA after he publicly declared that he was an avowed homosexual and a gay rights activist. Never mind asking why a practicing homosexual would want to lead a group whose mission is to teach young boys how to live morally straight, God-honoring lives, or why he would work his way up the ranks of a conservative organization only to drag them into court. Surely James was just an innocent victim, torn between his love of the scouts and his penchant for sodomy! (Had only Michael Jackson been so shrewd.)

The Supreme Court, in a 5-4 decision, held that the BSA has protection under the First Amendment to promote its own message and thus forbid homosexual leaders. Nevertheless, many citizens of Middle America were outraged by the "bigotry" of the Boy Scouts. The *Will and Grace* Club had once again bought the lie.

THE POLITICS OF HATE

The powerful influence of homosexuals, even in our impartial, "nonpolitical" court system, can not be ignored. (I expect a box full of hate mail and a few physical threats by the end of the month as always when I question anything gay. . . .)

Think for a minute about one of the most sensationalized cases of recent American history. No, football fans, not that one. And no, Billie Jean, not the more recent "Thriller" either. This case didn't even involve a celebrity. It involved a young man from Wyoming named Matthew Shepherd. Are you shocked that I mention it here as an example *against* the homosexual movement? Probably—if you believed everything the media reported on the case minus the complete set of facts.

Imagine my following conversation with the average gullible Moderate Middle American (MMA):

Me: *What was Matthew Shepherd the victim of?*
MMA: *A hate crime, of course.*

Me: *No. He was the victim of murder.*

MMA: *But the men who killed Matthew targeted him*
        because he was gay. That's a hate crime!

(Warning! Politically Incorrect Statement Ahead!)

Me: *So what if they targeted him because he was gay?*
        How is that different than if they murdered him for
        money or because he had slept with one of their
        wives?

MMA: *Because we have to stop all the discrimination and*
        hate in our country before any more gay, lesbian,
        bisexual, or transgendered people become victims!

Me: *The men who killed Matthew Shepherd—whatever*
        their motive—took away his Constitutional right to
        life. That is the issue at stake.

MMA: (exasperated) *I can't believe you are so intolerant!*

Me: (Raising voice, so the person storming away can
        hear) *Hey . . . at least try to see the 20/20 follow-up*
        report on this from 2004, where both of the killers
        and a lead investigator on the case said that drugs
        and money were their real motives. . . .

This imaginary conversation brings up an important point: *What in the world is a hate crime anyway?* How did we, a population of 42 percent Evangelicals, come to be so deluded in our thinking that we fell for the "hate crime" argument? Think about it—don't most crimes involve some level of malice? How is it *not* a hate crime when an employee kills his boss because he didn't give him a raise? Or when a woman kills her husband for cheating on her? When is hate not involved in any violent crime? The crime itself is the real issue, not the motive behind it.

Today's "free-thinking" gay activists want to make it illegal in the United States for anyone to speak against their lifestyle. A very large percentage of U.S. citizens agree with them. Where is the logic? On the social faux pas of smoking ciga-rettes, liberals (with the exception of onscreen celebrities) have taken quite the opposite tact. Following the logic of the homo-sexual movement, smokers should be protected instead of vili-fied, and anti-smoking ads would be banned as a violation of civil rights. *You've committed a hate crime, you smokophobe!* Besides, given the mere fact that the average lifespan of homo-sexuals is greatly reduced due to their sexual behavior, why *wouldn't* anyone want to seek treatment for an "alternative sex-ual preference"?

If you'll notice, hate crime legislation throughout the states did not come into full swing until the 1990s, well after the homosexual movement had established itself. But if there was any time period in our history when "hate crimes" would have had even an ounce of credence, it was during the civil rights movement of the late 1950s and 1960s. The thousands of beat-ings and lynchings faced by black Americans would easily qual-ify as a "hate crime" under today's standards.

Why then was such terminology propagated in the 90s instead? Because homosexual activists needed the forum of the courts to portray themselves as helpless "victims" in need of special protection from the hateful Christians. (By the way, it seems society's intolerance for "hateful language" leaves the building whenever anyone wants to denigrate Christians. And have you seen any popular television shows lately with a likable, intelligent Christian character? Or is there only room for the occasional religious psychomaniac or hypocrite? Can you believe that, not very long ago, it was not unusual for characters to pray on TV?)

Gays have been well-established as victims. But what about as perpetrators? When was the last time you heard any news reports on the number of sexual assaults or murders by homosexuals? Did any of the following crimes create the national hysteria of the Matthew Shepherd case? Did Katie Couric interview these victims' families?

- In 2001, two men were charged with the rape and murder of a boy in Arkansas.

- In 2002, a nineteen-year-old homosexual male murdered a fifty-one year-old Chicago Catholic woman for trying to convince him that he could change his lifestyle.

- In the 70s and 80s, the Lords of Bakersfield, a network of judges, executives, prosecutors, and newspaper men had homosexual sex with young boys and then used their power to cover up their tracks.

Unfortunately, the final case led to more crimes. In a series of stories that ran in January 2003, *The Bakersfield Californian* found evidence of a ring of closeted gay men who had sex with teenage boys and used their influence to keep from being prosecuted. Four of the men were slain between 1978 and 1984; in most of the cases, young men were charged with killing their suitors. The newspaper also revealed that its late publisher was a member of this homosexual conspiracy.

Sadly, there are many more crimes like the ones listed above, but in almost every case, the victim's story is suppressed by a media that is decidedly pro-homosexual rights. To test the theory of unequal reporting, Illinois Family Institute's Peter LaBarbera did a Nexis media search comparing the print media coverage on the Shepherd case with coverage on the murdered Chicago Catholic woman, Mary Stachowicz. In the three years following the day of her murder, "Mary Stachowicz" appeared in exactly twenty-five stories (including press releases and letters-to-the-editor) across our nation. When LaBarbera searched for stories containing "Matthew Shepard" over that same three-year period, the search engine interrupted itself because the list of documents had exceeded the 1,000-number limit. When he scaled the length of time back to the period between 11/04 and 11/05, Nexis produced 728 stories on the Shepard case. Many were newspaper articles about "The Laramie Project," a high school play that promotes the idea that Shepard's murder was a "hate crime" as a way of engendering pro-"gay" tolerance in schools.

Hmmm . . . I wonder if a play about the media's suppression of any negative publicity for homosexuals is in the works for our schoolchildren.

But enough about how the left discriminates among the worthiness of victims. Don't you want to know what happened to the Boy Scouts? Did the gaymaster triumph in court?

CALIFORNIA SCHEMIN' (AGAINST THE DREADED BOY SCOUTS)

In the year 2000, the Supreme Court (correctly) ruled in favor of the BSA, saying:

> That Boy Scouts, and all private organizations, have the constitutionally protected right under the First Amendment of freedom of association to set membership standards.

Score one for old-fashioned values and common sense! Unfortunately, the harassment against the Boy Scouts only intensified after that decision.

Back in the late 1980s, various youth organizations of San Diego requested that the city lease a half-acre piece of land in Mission Bay to the Boy Scouts. The Boy Scouts wanted to build an aquatic center that would be available for use by all of the city's youth groups and any other organization. The city agreed and entered into a lease with the BSA. At a cost of two-and-a-half million dollars, the BSA funded the center with its own resources, using no public money. Even though most groups who frequent the center are unaffiliated with the Boy Scouts, BSA underwrites all of the aquatic center's operating losses.

Rewind to the 1950s, when the city asked the Boy Scouts, the Girl Scouts, and Campfire to develop and operate a remote part of Balboa Park for youth camping. Just as with the aquatic center, these camping facilities are often used by youth organizations not affiliated with the BSA.

In 2001, San Diego renewed both of these leases with the Boy Scouts and Girl Scouts for another twenty-five years with the provision that the groups would invest another one-and-a-half million dollars in both of the properties. Each year, the BSA already underwrites a total of one hundred and fifty thousand dollars in maintenance costs for both the aquatic center and the camping facilities at no cost to the taxpayer of San Diego County.

I know what you are thinking. With such a blatant history of community service, it's a wonder they were not sued sooner! So what is this lawsuit about?

In a perfect model of legal frivolity, the suit, filed by a lesbian couple and an agnostic couple (shocking!), alleges that the city of San Diego violated the California and federal Constitutions by leasing parkland to the Scouts—land they have used since 1946. Incredibly the judge of this particular case, U.S. District Judge Napoleon A. Jones, Jr., found in favor of the plaintiffs, citing that the city had given the Boy Scouts preferential treatment since the BSA did not participate in a competitive bidding process.

Surely he jests. Competitive bidding process for a private organization to spend their own money on a public facility? Jones also ruled that the Balboa lease violated the constitutional separation of church and state, concluding there was "over-whelming and uncontradicted evidence" showing that the Boy Scouts of America is a religious organization.

Obviously the judge's "impartial" reasoning veiled the true sentiments of a "public servant" who used his judicial power to advance his own liberal bias. Confirming this, in his closing comments, Jones slammed the Boy Scouts as "anti-homosexual . . .

anti-atheist," and "at odds with values requiring tolerance and inclusion in the public realm." (Ah, the ultimate values of tolerance and inclusion.)

The American Civil Liberties Union (ACLU) claimed that the city's lease renewal with the Boy Scouts was another example of the discriminatory policies that began all the way back in the 1950s when San Diego first reached out to the BSA. Their position perfectly demonstrates how the far-left bullies it way through the courts. They throw out provocative terms meant to insinuate that someone is being denied something that he or she has every right to have.

Certainly the Boy Scouts were not trying to make a social statement against gays and lesbians when they first began making improvements on public property. The homosexual movement hadn't truly begun in earnest, yet the BSA went looking for a fight with a fringe subculture that was, at best, less than 3 percent of the population? No, the Boy Scouts simply wanted to improve San Diego's public parks in fulfillment of part of the Boy Scout pledge—to serve the community.

A similar case popped up in Berkeley, California, when the city allowed other non-profit organization free use of the city marina . . . except the Sea Scouts, "a Boy Scout affiliate that focuses on sailing." Ignoring First Amendment protection of the "free association of individuals," city leaders denounced the Sea Scouts as, you guessed it, "discriminatory." A city that discriminates against the Boy Scouts—or any other organization—for its moral stance is both hypocritical and unconstitutional. City governments are supposed to uphold the Constitution, not marginalize groups and individuals whose policies annoy them.

Heck, the KKK gets more respect from our state governments than the Boy Scouts do!

I bring up these cases involving the BSA not because I want you to give them an encouraging salute next time you see them or write them a fat check of support (although both would be nice). Rather, I include these incredible accounts here to remind Middle America how powerful those "crazy lefties" have become in our society. While we were watching *Seinfeld*, liberals turned logic into "hate crimes," irrationality into "sound social theory," and immorality into Constitutionally-protected activity. This is cause for alarm.

If Boy Scouts can be vilified, none of us are safe.

THE EARTHQUAKE OF '73

Some verdicts from America's liberal courts are downright funny in their absurdity. Other verdicts are positively evil.

When the Supreme Court ruled in 1973 that abortion is a private matter, that no public standard exists relevant to the question of a woman destroying her own fetus, they officially cut the umbilical cord, so to speak, that connected the private individual to any prevailing moral or social standards associated with the consequences of sexual behavior.

In our country's history, our sense of the sacred had defined the way we related to life and death. *Roe v. Wade* shifted that view, saying that, as a society, we see no sacred component to sex, or to its natural consequences. With a stroke of a judge's pen, the idea of holding something sacred was banished from our public life.

Roe v. Wade sent a strong message to our culture. Much of the devaluing of life today among criminals, young people, and even the far-left of the medical community can be traced back to this decision.

In brief, what message did the Supreme Court send Americans in 1973?

- Legal abortion on demand sent a clear, sad message about our nation's cultural attitude to life and its value. If society doesn't protect its most vulnerable, why should its citizens protect other members of society who don't have obvious "material value"?

- The fact that this message was federalized by the Supreme Court, pre-empting states, established this "right" as a transcendent national value. It wasn't just some lefties in California condoning abortion; the endorsement was "official."

- The "right to privacy," which served as the foundational argument for *Roe v. Wade,* enshrined relativism as a central cultural and legal national reality. If my individual rights trump objective morality, I can excuse any action I take in the name of freedom of choice.

The legal earthquake of '73 left a landscape of moral wreckage and ethical aftershocks. Buried in the rubble was the "old-fashioned" concept of an objective right and wrong. Over thirty years later, how does our scarred nation feel about *Roe v. Wade?*

- Fifty-one percent of Americans say that abortion is "morally wrong."

- Sixty-three percent of Americans support *Roe v. Wade*.

- Twenty-three percent of Americans support legal abortion "under any circumstances."

- The majority of abortion supporters feel it should be legal "only in a few circumstances."

Both sides in the abortion debate could find hope for their cause in this data. What it tells me is that even if most people believe in a woman's "right to choose," America does not support the spirit of *Roe v. Wade*. Under the decision, the legalization of abortion was based on the rationale of a principle called the "right to privacy." However, if most Americans agreed that abortion is legal because of a person's fundamental right to do it, they would not respond in polls saying that abortion is immoral and should be legal "only in a few circumstances."

The fact that most Americans see abortion as immoral, and that the legal foundation for abortion is tenuous at best, reveals the underlying discomfort nationwide with today's legal regime that governs abortion. These sentiments were expressed when we elected a conservative Republican president and a Republican congress.

Although abortion has affected Americans from every level of society, the devaluing of life and its concurrent stance that objective truths do not exist disproportionately hurts communities that already face great social and cultural challenges. The black community, deeply damaged since the 1960s by the culture of the welfare state, has come to be defined by the destructive relativism at the root of *Roe v. Wade.* The lack of a moral compass has torn apart black families.

Today, seven of ten black babies are born to unwed mothers. Those seven babies will, in all likelihood, grow up in an environment where, wherever they turn—home, school, their neighborhood, television and music, and even the laws of their country—the message they will hear is that whatever they feel like doing is okay. If a young woman wants to sleep around, that's up to her. If she wants to abort the results of her liaison, also her call. As for the young man who fathers and abandons several children, why not? With no moral absolutes, there are no societal limits on behavior. We have lost more than our regard for the value of life. We have lost a common decency. We have lost our sense of shame.

CONSENTING ADULTS

The liberal latitude in our courtrooms today has serious implications. Without a common moral code, irrational theories and half-truths begin to sound reasonable until they are "unofficial" societal standards. These standards become law when liberal citizens file complaints and activist judges apply broad interpretation to sanction them.

The cycle goes something like this: An atheist in Oregon finds out that her elementary child is to sing "Silent Night" at a Christmas concert, files an official lawsuit against the school, and the end result is that my local courthouse can't display a nativity scene, and your son can't pray at his high school graduation. Just one easily offended person who is willing to raise a fuss can change the daily lives of the whole nation (as long as that person is offended by something like prayer or a Christmas tree and not constitutionally protected material like pornography, homosexual expression, or abortion).

One frightening example of how both morality and common sense can be left behind in the dust of a progressive legal system is the "consenting adults" argument.

People living in the twenty-first century have certainly heard that line of reasoning to justify a variety of behaviors: "_____ is okay as long as it's between consenting adults in the privacy of their own home. After all, that's their First Amendment right!" Anyone who disagrees that the Constitution protects whatever-the-liberal-establishment-wants-it-to is viewed as either a bigot or a Neanderthal.

A modern application of the consenting adults argument was the Supreme Court's 2003 decision on *Lawrence v. Texas,* which struck down Texas's anti-sodomy laws. The majority decision found that "the intimate, adult consensual conduct at issue here was part of the liberty protected by the substantive component of the Fourteenth Amendment's due process protections." (The First Amendment is not the only helpful tool, you know.) Justice Kennedy's opinion specified that the right of consenting adults to have sex was based on on how intimate and personal the conduct was to those involved, not on whether the conduct was traditionally protected by society (as if that's an issue anymore), or conducted by married people. One Web site discussed the potential moral fallout from the ruling:

It opened the door in theory to protection of a whole host of sexual activity between consenting adults not protected by other decisions. The Court has not ruled on statutes prohibiting adult incest, polygamy, adultery, prostitution, and other forms of sexual intimacy between consenting adults. *Lawrence* may have created a slippery slope for these laws to eventually fall.

Texas Congressman Dr. Ron Paul said this about the skewed legal logic behind the case:

Ridiculous as sodomy laws may be, there clearly is no right to privacy nor sodomy found anywhere in the Constitution. There are, however, *states' rights*—rights plainly affirmed in the Ninth and Tenth Amendments. Under those amendments, the State of Texas has the right to decide for itself how to regulate social matters like sex, using its own local standards. But rather than applying the real Constitution and declining jurisdiction over a properly state matter, the Court decided to apply the imaginary Constitution.

He went on to discuss that year's other applications of the "imaginary Constitution":

From "gay rights" to affirmative action to Boy Scouts to the Ten Commandments, federal courts recently have issued rulings that conflict with both the Constitution and overwhelming public sentiment. Conservatives and libertarians who once viewed the judiciary as the final bulwark against government tyranny must now accept that no branch of government even remotely performs its constitutional role. . . . With the federal judiciary focused more on promoting a social agenda than upholding the rule of law, Americans find themselves increasingly governed by men they did not elect and cannot remove from office. . . . The political left increasingly uses the federal judiciary to do in court what it cannot do at the ballot box: advance an activist, secular, multicultural political agenda of which most Americans disapprove.

(Representative Paul is dead-on about the way liberals have taken over our court system. I pray he is correct that "most Americans" disapprove of their agenda.)

No Constitutional scholar worth his salt will ever defend the complete license to do anything in the privacy of one's own home—that's urban legend that has been propagated by James Carville ever since his buddy Bill got caught in White House humidor. If privacy protected everything, local judges could never obtain a search warrant to look for illegal paraphernalia.

But secondly, and more importantly, the whole "consenting adults" argument is a fantasy invented by little fairies in the minds of college professors who have way too much time on their hands. Think about the implications of this argument if applied to its extreme, as it already is in other nations. This year in the Netherlands, three consenting adults (a male heterosexual and his two bisexual "wives") were joined in a civil union. Wouldn't that make for an interesting "family" sitcom! And what about those countries where the "age of consent" is as low as twelve or the states where it is fourteen? Add to the mix legal prostitution and we could conceivably see a day where child prostitution is legal in our country. Who knows what perverted fantasies may become "constitutional" if the liberal agenda continues to unravel the moral fiber of our country?

If you think I'm overreacting or paranoid, read this true, stranger-than-even-science-fiction account which shows just how far the whole "consenting adults" mindset has taken the terminally depraved of one country. A few years ago, a German man placed an ad on the Internet for a "young, well-built man who wants to be eaten." Incredibly, someone responded to the ad, came to the man's house, and proceeded to allow the man to actually carve him up and eat him, even while he was still alive! In the end, the murderer was sentenced to only eight and a half years in prison.

While the story is shocking enough, what's more unsettling is that many Europeans came to the defense of the murderer because the act took place between two consenting adults! In fact, the familiar adage, "to each his own," was the man's primary defense! The deceased had agreed to be killed and eaten, and the defendant was more than willing to satisfy his wishes, so what was the problem? This same argument is used to justify all kinds of perversions, and with a straight face. Lunacy is the end result of a radicalized freedom between consenting adults. Charles Colson, in his article "Consenting Adults: Responding to a Cannibal," writes:

Perhaps the secularist could say that he finds killing and cannibalism repulsive. But that's no argument. Some pro-choice activists, when pressed, will admit that they find a procedure like partial-birth abortion repulsive. But they'll fight for it because they believe any restrictions on abortions are a blow to their personal autonomy. So how can they object to the way these two men exercised their personal autonomy, even if it was repulsive?

In the mind of a true liberal, the following statement makes complete sense: You can eat another person who consents to it, but you can't smoke in a public restaurant.

And one group whose focus is the issue of consent is the North American Man/Boy Love Association. Of course, this high-minded group cares more about "consenting kids" than adults. NAMBLA posted this on its Web site:

> Our goal is to end the oppression of men and boys who have freely chosen mutually *consensual* relationships. [emphasis mine]

The organization adds that "NAMBLA is strongly opposed to age-of-consent laws and all other restrictions which deny men and boys the full enjoyment of their bodies and control over their own lives." So as long as the act is consensual, it is acceptable and should be protected, whether that act is murder, cannibalism, or child rape.

That is the final conclusion of a society who believes that liberty has no limits.

WHAT'S THE MATTER
WITH AMERICA?

At the beginning of this chapter I referred to Thomas Frank's controversial book *What's the Matter with Kansas? How Conservatives Won the Heart of America.* In it, he discusses what really separates right and left America:

> It is cultural issues that most divide the nation . . . on cultural matters; they [Americans] are radically at odds with one another. The differences in their realms of moral understanding go so deep as to make communication difficult. Their mutual incomprehension produces stereotypes of the other that range from the oversimplified to the truly vicious. . . . At its deepest level this is a war of religion.

Although Frank represents "The Other Side," I agree with his assessment that America's political conflicts mask a deeper battle over core values. The cultural war cuts across all racial and economic boundaries. This is not the class warfare that has been propagated by the far left for the last five decades. This is a war between right and wrong, one that has been fought in different forms since the beginning of time.

Today's liberal politicians and journalists not only pit the generous Democrats against the mean-spirited conservative Republicans, they attempt to alienate and stigmatize Americans who respect traditional values and Judeo Christian beliefs as being uncaring, "un-American" radicals.

Their insistence on individual freedom has led to freedom from individual responsibility. What they fail to grasp is that an America free from moral restraint is not truly free. Does anyone think that the people trapped in their attics after Lake Ponchatrain flooded New Orleans had freedom? Of course not. In the aftermath of a horrible disaster, those unfortunate individuals had no where else to go, not because of the Bush Administration or FEMA or Governor Blanco or Mayor Nagin, but because of their own past decisions. For years, some had ignored the call to evacuate a doomed lifestyle. For days, others had ignored the call to evacuate a doomed city.

The tenets of freedom are rooted in traditional morality. Middle America must be clear about what the rules of humanity are and then defend them without compromise.

FAITH
IN THE
GHETTO

Religion in America is under attack. Or at least 64 percent of the 800 Americans polled in October 2005 think so. That number rose to 80 percent if the respondent was an evangelical, fundamental, or charismatic Christian. A majority also agreed that religion is "losing" influence in American life.

Those statistics do not surprise Father Richard John Neuhaus. He coined the term the "naked public square" to describe the marketplace of ideas in our country that has excused God from the dialogue. Little by little, the liberal religion of secularism has tried to remove God and religion from schools, neighborhoods, television, movies, government, the Pledge of Allegiance, and even our own homes. And with much success. God has been "dead and buried" to many radicals for decades. The remaining task is to remove the last vestiges of His presence from society.

My bishop once told me an interesting story that gives credence to the theory of the naked public square. When he first moved to a new suburb in Orange County, he heard what sounded like church bells ringing in the middle of the "town." (There are no real towns in Southern California, just several "parkways" with apartment buildings fixed around them.) On a jog one day, he determined to find the church. He looked and looked, but no steeple. When he finally located the source of the mysterious bells, the "church" he'd been seeking turned out to be the local community center! He then started looking for any church in the area, and to his amazement, he found none—at least not close-by. When he did find the local churches, they appeared incognito, on a backstreet behind a large wall shielding them from view. God and his religious fanatics had been relegated to the boondocks.

Orange Countians are not the only ones too sophisticated for God. On the East coast, a planned neighborhood in Maryland included in its charter a provision prohibiting the establishment of a church anywhere within its borders. Such hostility toward God when just a few decades ago, city planners not only made room for a church, but set aside property in the center of the town for it!

Have ordinary Americans in fact become anti-religious? On the contrary, most Americans still profess to believe in God or a Supreme Being. A very large percentage of U.S. citizens say they are Protestant, and many of those claim to be Evangelicals. Yet people give a bizarre mix of opinions on issues of morality like homosexual marriage and abortion. With moral confusion and contempt for religion on the rise in our nation, I must ask: *How did the land of "one nation under God" arrive at this godless place?*

Many in Middle America will point the finger at Hollywood and Washington for our nation's moral collapse. This is not without reason: Mel Gibson had to fund his own *The Passion of the Christ* while the Academy Awards rolled out the red carpet for *Million Dollar Baby* and Roman Polanski. The same U. S. Supreme Court that banned the posting of the Ten Commandments on government property found Texas's anti-sodomy laws unconstitutional, opening a floodgate of homosexual activism. With each passing year, Hollywood productions and D.C. rulings seem to grow more illogical and morally perverse. (As I write this, the newest gem from Hollywood is a "groundbreaking romance," the gay cowboy movie, *Brokeback Mountain*. To no one's surprise, the critics are raving.)

Yet, the moral mudbath in which we find ourselves is not solely the fault of lascivious producers and calculating judges. The entertainment and the politics of Hollywood and D.C. didn't just spring up on their own. There has to be an impetus, something which has driven and still drives producers and politicians, writers, and legislators to create movies and pass laws that disdain religious tradition and encourage moral contempt. That impetus is called the market.

In other words, it is us.

TABOOS WITH A PURPOSE

For hundreds and thousands of years, truth as prescribed by religious tradition dominated society. People from every culture and religion recognized that maintaining traditional cultural and tribal beliefs was crucial for preserving the family and community. For example, adultery and divorce were both considered absolutely taboo. Why? Because both led to the breakdown of the family, the most stabilizing unit in society. Early cultures knew that when the family breaks down, children do not learn how to survive on their own, care for their young, or earn an income. In short, the society that allows rampant adultery and divorce quickly loses its moorings, threatening its own future. This perhaps explains why adultery was at one time punishable by death.

Unlike the radical individualism of our time that espouses complete freedom—vulgar, complacent, sexual, and otherwise—the people who began our nation well understood the dangers of unchecked passions. Conservative scholar Russell Kirk praised the moral structures laid down by America's early leaders. He said they knew that mankind, given his base nature, "must put a control upon his will and his appetite . . . man [is] governed more by emotion than by reason. Tradition and sound prejudice provide checks upon man's anarchic impulse."

With that said, Christianity has always recognized the natural proclivity of humanity to gravitate toward the lowest common denominator of its base nature. Unlike the animal kingdom whose members are subject to instinct for organization, control, and survival, human beings are easily given to individual passions which, left unchecked, lead to despotism or savagery. This is why the Puritans were so obsessed with legislating and maintaining moral purity throughout their communities—they knew firsthand the negative effects of unrestrained passions running wild in both church and society.

It is also the reason why the founding fathers were sure to incorporate a system of checks and balances within the U.S. Constitution. They understood man's tendency for acquiring and abusing power; they had witnessed it firsthand while under the rule of George III. Hard experience had given them the wisdom to know that they themselves were capable of the same crimes perpetrated by the English monarchy.

FAITH OF OUR FATHERS

The argument over whether the United States was founded on Christian principles has gone on for decades with little or no resolution. Liberals quote James Madison and John Stuart Mill as evidence that the founding fathers had no intention of allowing religion, Christianity to be specific, to have any influence on the writing of the Constitution, the Bill of Rights, or any foundational aspect of our democratic republic. Conservatives point to George Washington and other Christian signers of the Constitution as clear guardians of Biblical truth in its relationship to government.

Clearly the most controversial figure in the debate is Thomas Jefferson, writer of the Declaration of Independence. Jefferson took issues of morality very seriously. He was a deist, but had a clear understanding and appreciation for Judeo Christian morality outlined in the Bible. Although he disregarded any reference to Christ being God incarnate, he held firm convictions on the ethical and moral teachings of Jesus the man. He shrewdly observed that the religious groups of his time may have battled over doctrinal issues, but they agreed that basic Judeo Christian morality was immutable.

Jefferson's noble words are etched into the minds of most Americans. As the slave owner who penned them, he must have had an understanding of universal morality even beyond himself:

> We hold these truths to be self-evident, that all men are created equal, that they are endowed by their Creator with certain unalienable rights, that among these are Life, Liberty, and the pursuit of Happiness.

(In the first drafts of the Declaration, men's unalienable rights were listed as "Life, Liberty, and the pursuit of *Property*." Early

Americans believed property carried greater value than its material worth. As the guarantor of all other rights, it represented not just a man's accumulation of wealth, but his life's opportunity and security. Regardless of what many tenured socialist professors convey to the itching ears of their idealistic students, capital—money and property—is a requirement for securing one's family, health, and future. Just ask Rep. Nancy Pelosi [D-CA] how far she would have gone in securing her bid for the House of Representatives if not for "Property.")

Many Americans today pursue "Happiness" brazenly. But, contrary to "anything goes" advocates, Jefferson never intended this pursuit to lead to reckless abandon. The meticulous scholar attributed the gift of this right to man's Creator. Viewed in historical context, the phrase "the pursuit of Happiness" can only mean happiness within the moral context of the Judeo Christian ethic that the framers' Western heritage gave them.

True social deconstructionists disagree, urging an interpretation of the Declaration and the Constitution outside of their historical context. However, one of their favorite founders, James Madison, whom they often quote in defense of a strict separation of church and state, said this about interpreting texts:

> Do not separate text from historical background. If you do, you will have perverted and subverted the Constitution, which can only end in a distorted, bastardized form of illegitimate government.

Hard to find any ambiguity of meaning in that. It is also hard to see how those seeking to quash "all things religious" from public society can disregard John Adams' assertion that:

> We have no government armed with power capable of
> contending with human passions unbridled by morality
> and religion. . . . Our Constitution was made only for a
> moral and religious people. It is wholly inadequate to
> the government of any other.

Our forefathers recognized that basic liberty, supported by faith
in an unseen God, gives a person the potential to be free to
make his own decisions without intrusion from governmental
tyranny—the exact thing they sought to escape during the days
of the Revolution. Biblical values and liberty are inextricably
linked. Indeed, to separate the two would be to sound the death
knell for our American Republic.

Even so, swayed by legions of liberals hailing the importance of the "separation of church and state," (a phrase which
never appears in the Constitution, by the way) many Middle
Americans carry the misperception that our nation's foundation of freedom *of* religion is actually freedom *from* religion.
Our forefathers denounced the oppression of a pervasive, all-
encompassing and limiting state religion; they did not dismiss
anything smacking of holiness. Knowing the values of America's
first citizens, it is hard to see how those championing the
removal of every iota of religion from the public sphere call
themselves historically accurate, or even patriotic. They certainly do not respect our true heritage. In his farewell speech of
1796, President George Washington wrote:

> Of all dispositions and habits which lead to political
> prosperity, religion and morality are indispensable

supports. . . . And let us with caution indulge the sup-
position, that morality can be maintained without religion . . . reason and experience forbid us to expect that
national morality can prevail in exclusion of religious
principle. 'Tis substantially true, that virtue or morality
is a necessary spring of popular government.

And liberals justify removing the star off the community
Christmas tree in the spirit of our heritage of freedom? Hardly.
The early fathers fled the tyranny of the Church of England for
freedom. We have fled religious freedom for the tyranny of
secularism.

THEIR CHILDREN'S "PROGRESS": A COUNTRY RULED BY "ISMS"

When did the uniting common denominator of Judeo-
Christian morals begin to end? Fast forward from the time of
our nation's birth to the mid-1800s, when a group of European
thinkers, writers, and poets decided to revise the traditional
notion of sin. They preached the perfectibility of man through
meditation and reflection on nature, saying mankind did not
need redemption from sin as offered by traditional Christian
beliefs. These ill winds of change blew across the ocean and into
our borders, forever altering American culture.

As the Industrial Revolution erupted and "modern science"
demolished ancient "truths," America underwent a frightening
transformation in its political and social philosophy. The growing faith in science and technology made the average American
believe anything was possible—and permissible. New inven-

tions and new fortunes popped up daily, bringing fame and fortune to a people more attuned to forging through the rugged frontier than through the trappings of modern living. Medical advancements gave new hope to yesterday's doomed cases. Some radicals even shed the "encumbrances" of religion, dreaming of man's capability to perfect himself. The Progressive Movement had begun.

The truth-as-prescribed-by-science explosion was a relatively new concept, the direct result of the earlier Enlightenment of the mid-1600s through the 1700s. Enlightened believers exalted the power of science to answer all the mysteries of life. No longer were scientific discoveries tempered by religious tradition. Thanks to the groundswell of materialism in Europe, formerly taboo questions became en vogue. Matters of "facts" eventually overtook matters of "faith" in this high-charged laboratory of ideas. The Enlightenment gained influence over every arena of life, most notably in politics and religion. After centuries of "oppressive" Christianity, atheism and agnosticism were now fashionable.

The enlightened idea of trashing religious bonds to pursue a higher way—namely, to do whatever you feel like doing—has taken on many names. By the dictates of vocabulary, most of these philosophies end with an "ism": progressivism, secularism, modernism, post modernism, atheism, agnosticism, nihilism, materialism . . . the *isms* parade marches through history. Though each group embracing its particular *ism* sees itself as innovative and revolutionary, in reality men and women have been choosing their desires over God's laws since the Fall of Man. (Ever heard of Forbidden-Fruitism?)

Moral relativism has been Middle America's most recent *ism* of rebellion, spurred on by materialism and progressivism, and melding neatly with secularism. (The *isms* humorously blend together into philosophical mush after years of diatribes and tributes, but their overall effect is no joke.) Moral relativism is a belief system in which morality is fluid, changeable, and based upon each individual's view of the world. A belief in moral relativism requires that every person respects each individual's right to his or her own morality, regardless of how bizarre or how dangerous it might be.

I could search for a better definition, but thankfully, I don't have to. In 1992, Justice Kennedy, writing for the majority opinion in *Planned Parenthood v. Casey*, stated, "At the heart of liberty is the right to define one's own concept of existence, of meaning, of the universe, and of the mystery of human life." In one sentence, Kennedy explained quite succinctly the motto of moral relativism.

Unfortunately, many in Middle America would find Kennedy's words more generous than dangerous. After all, we are big on the rights we have as citizens. The majority of us would not want to be accused of impinging upon a person's rights to live as he or she chooses. Even more, we do not want our own "rights" violated by others.

WHO CAN OBJECT WITHOUT OBJECTIVE TRUTH?

The fact that our compulsion regarding rights is driven by a feeling rather than a truth is a problem. But what compels us to feel this way? Why are we so willing to acquiesce to such a watered-down and distorted version of the liberty secured with the blood, sweat, and tears of our forefathers?

Perhaps we are deceived because when the philosophy of materialism (relativism's uncle) makes gains in any culture or society, the first casualties are objective reason and truth. Materialism says that everything that occurs in the universe, even those seemingly unexplained mysteries, is strictly the result of chemical and physical reactions. If all of "consciousness is but the static emanating from the three pounds of meat that is the brain," then objectivity is lost. Nothing can be agreed upon in terms of law, justice, truth, or reason, for these are just the irrational products of biology, genetics, and environment.

For example, many Americans believe in God and that He hears and answers prayers. The materialist, however, would argue that belief in God and the power of prayer is naturally the result of a highly-evolved human brain. Even scientific evidence that belief in God and prayer enhances the health of those who practice these disciplines is explained away as the "God compartment" of the Judeo Christian belief in the soul. Eternal life can be reduced down to a few chemicals acting in such a way as to produce religious feelings.

In terms of personal responsibility, materialism allows its believers to defer blame to anyone or anything besides themselves. A society that derives its notions of truth from a strictly materialist view thrusts all kinds of wickedness upon its culture and turns justice upside down. This is why some liberals dared to blame the United States for the Al Qaeda terrorist attacks on the World Trade Center buildings.

Whether Middle America realizes it or not, both religious and nonreligious Americans are infected to some degree with the materialist philosophy. Over time, scientific skepticism has crept into our thoughts and made itself permanently at home. While we won't actually profess a devotion to materialism, its belief system works like a virus affecting the daily decisions we make about education, marriage, religion, health, and love. Some of us try hard to fight off its effects; most either don't know the virus is present or just plain don't care.

For their part, materialists have a very difficult time understanding spiritual concepts or relating to a biblical perception of life because they believe all mysteries of the universe will be solved through empirical science and the power of the microscope. Since various physicists have declared that there is no room for God in the universe, there is no room for antiquated religious dogma that restricts the progress or freedom of mankind either. This rejection of God sterilizes their view of the human race.

In his novel *That Hideous Strength,* the great philosopher C.S. Lewis shows how easily highly educated men and women can be seduced into this kind of nonsense. The main character, Mark Studdock, goes to work for a secretive scientific foundation called the National Institute for Coordinated Experiments, or N.I.C.E. Of course, the institute is anything but nice. Through funding by the national government, N.I.C.E. commits horrible acts on human beings, all in the name of scientific progression. Another main character, a scientist working for the institute, sums up the institute's worldview in this manner:

"Before going on," said Frost, "I must ask you to be strictly objective. Resentment and fear are both chemical phenomena. Our reactions to one another are chemical phenomena. Social relations are chemical reactions. You must observe these feelings in yourself in an objective manner. Do not let them distract your attention from the facts."

What does he mean by *objective*? He means to remain objective about the fact that all of man's perceived reality is strictly the product of brain function. But how can a person be objective if there is no basis for objective truth? In the end, what do you have left? By reducing all of our perceptions of right and wrong down to a few electrical charges, truth and reason become the blown fuses of a short-circuited philosophy.

Millions of Americans have been seduced into trading their God-given purpose and eternal perspective for a materialistic worldview that strips them of their hearts and souls. For example, although a substantial percentage of the U.S. population claims to be Christian, far too many also believe in the theory of evolution.

A firestorm erupted in 2005 over whether the theory of intelligent design should be taught in science classes along with the theory of evolution. Intelligent design poses the hypothesis that since the universe is so complex, it must have been created by a higher being. Yet renowned scientists across our country have convinced many in middle-class America to choose a more "scientifically sound" option:

There was nothing. Nothing. Nothing. (So far, Creationists

agree). And then all of a sudden for no apparent reason, BANG! Life started. Of course, we weren't as sophisticated as we are now—we used to be monkeys, and birds were dinosaurs, but, by amazing time and chance, our detailed, intricate world has grown to be more detailed and intricate.

By denying the role of God in creation, society, and our personal lives, we are robbing ourselves of one of His precious gifts: our immeasurable human worth. Since we are just the products of biology, there is no intrinsic beauty or goodness in anything. We are left to find our value in our accomplishments or others' approval. After all, without a Divine Creator, an object can only have beauty if judged well by "the eye of the beholder."

SCIENCE AS GOD

Is middle-class America immune from the effects of the Enlightenment? Consider that most Americans, Christian and non-Christian alike, hang on every word that comes from the scientific community. Flannery O'Connor once commented about the state of American culture in the 1950s by saying that our society believes that all the mysteries of life will fall under the power of the microscope.

It is quite difficult today to find a group of more than three people who agree on the most fundamental of beliefs. And if you're the odd man out (oops, I mean "odd *person* out") in a public sphere like a university classroom and you happen to profess the same fundamental beliefs on morality as Jefferson and Washington held, you're likely to be shouted down with highly emotional rhetoric and accused of being intolerant, cruel, or just plain dumb.

Reverence for God has no place in the minds of a substantial percentage of contemporary America's three hundred million citizens, many of whom daily exalt the sacrosanct "personal opinion" as god in every Internet chat room and local coffee shop.

How far has materialism pervaded our thought processes? It certainly has lowered our perception of the value of life. Violence fills our televisions, music, computer games, and unfortunately, our inner city-culture. A look at the low-income, minority neighborhoods of cities such as Atlanta, Chicago, and New York City gives us a revealing slice of the all-American pie of values: One city in south-central Los Angeles had a homicide rate ten times that of the national average in 2004. Detroit, with its impoverished downtown section, is listed by Morgan Quitno as the second most dangerous city to live in the United States. Geographical location, however, does not guarantee a person safety from the callous bullet: most of the tragic school shootings in our country have occurred in rural, white Middle America.

Our enlightened nation is hell-bent on believing the ludicrous and rejecting the rationally sane. And our enlightenment is taking us down the toilet. Here are some random symptoms of a morally sick society, one that has traded faith for facts, and facts for fiction:

- Eleven percent of Americans believe there should be no restrictions on embryonic stem-cell research;

42 percent want the president to ease restrictions. This means a simple majority believes that research on stem-cells obtained from human embryos should be allowed in the United States.

- In past days, Americans sought guidance from the clergy, trusted community elders, wise family members, and God Himself. Today we seek help from psychiatrists, Prozac, *Cosmopolitan* magazine, Oprah, Dr. Phil, and on occasion, Tom Cruise.

- In the world of literature, millions upon millions of middle-class Americans bought and devoured *The Da Vinci Code* as though it had been penned by Jesus Christ Himself.

- *Caveat:* The use of science as our moral foundation is suspended when politically incorrect. For example, research has shown that women who have had an abortion have a significantly increased risk for breast and ovarian cancer, along with psychological problems stemming from guilt for killing their child. Practicing homosexuality greatly increases your chances of contracting a disease. But neither of these behaviors is condemned in popular society today as much as smoking.

In their crusade to replace the spiritual with the material, materialists have failed to grasp what most ordinary Americans do: life is more than just a mass of elements, water, and neurons. Yes, the fruits we harvest today from freedom and technology are great. But if our society is to flourish, we must recover a sense of responsibility commensurate with the freedom and power we now possess.

A HOLY HERITAGE OF FREEDOM

Make no mistake—there is no such thing as a value-free or religion-free society. It is impossible to live in a vacuum, free from the influence of moral belief.

As creatures who need boundaries, we most often seek these boundaries to be defined by those who are in authority—the experts, so to speak. With each new generation, a new group is elected or nominated to act as the political, religious, and moral authority of their generation.

Some of these cultural leaders do not seem to understand the gravity of their role.

Why else would Nancy Pelosi, Ward Churchill, and Al Franken proclaim that allowing religion to affect public policy will only invite discrimination and violence? Do these leaders not know their history?

If public schools taught the true, nonpolitically correct version of history, our students might know the ominous truth: every civilization that has entered a period of moral collapse has opened the door to other social ills (heightened criminal activity, eating disorders, and physical ailments from illicit sex) and moral anarchy that invites power-hungry public officials to impose martial law and eventually rule by tyranny. Unless a society recognizes its error and turns away from this course, moral dissipation always leads to the end of that civilization, regardless of its size or strength.

Contrary to radical pundits' assertions, the history of Judeo Christian morality resounds with sweeping political and social changes in the growth of liberty. After Christ ascended into heaven and the church was just getting started, Christian doctrine proclaimed liberty to an array of distinct social classes, classes similar to the ones found in India today. Prior to the advent of Christianity, women in the Roman Empire were considered second-class citizens, and slaves could be killed at the whim of their masters. Life was extremely dismal for the majority of people living during this time period, but Christianity, with its radically new teaching that men and women should love their neighbors as they love themselves, gave hope to all those whose unalienable rights had been trampled upon. Some of Christ's most loyal disciples were women; many of them had been forgiven of sins that could have landed them in prison or even led to their deaths—all under the authority of the law of the land.

Although slavery still existed in most quarters of Europe for the next several centuries, the seeds of liberty planted by Christianity continued to grow. Eventually they yielded fruit in Great Britain, and then in the United States. The Abolitionist movement, for instance, was started by Christians whose consciences would not allow them to abide by the law of slavery in the United States. Many of them gave up their livelihoods and their lives in defense of the African slave and his right to Life, Liberty, and the pursuit of Happiness.

In Europe, it was Christianity that motivated Parliament leader William Wilberforce to lead the first campaign to abolish the slave trade and slavery in the British Empire. The famous Christian hymn *Amazing Grace* was written by a British slave trader named John Newton after he converted to Christianity, denounced his former profession, and became a clergyman.

In view of these facts, the claims academic elites and power-driven politicians make against Christianity in the public square are disingenuous, irrational, and just plain wrong. Have these "patriots" forgotten the early days of our nation, when every colony desiring statehood made sure to include at least one reference to God in its state constitution?

Would acknowledging Christianity in our public forums truly ignite hatred and bigotry as they claim? Our nation used to be composed of states with an overwhelming majority of citizens devoted to the precepts of Judeo Christian morality. And, yet, these same states opened up their doors to all kinds of people from a variety of countries, races, ethnicities, and religious backgrounds. Would the mass wave of immigrants have come to our shores during the 1800s if our Christian nation welcomed them with religious bigotry and violence? Would they have sought our haven of liberty if we oppressed them with religion?

Certainly there were problems. Some immigrants faced prejudice and resentment over their presence and strange customs. But the fact remains, during a time when most Americans unashamedly lived out biblical morality and proclaimed their faith in God and Jesus Christ, an enormous group of humanity chose our country as a guaranteed refuge of freedom.

This fact doesn't square with the inane rhetoric of many of today's popular social engineers and politicians, who paint a very grim picture of the Christian religion.

If you don't think that America was highly influenced by Biblical teachings, look at the public school system prior to the Scopes Trials and John Dewey. Creationism was the *only* "theory" on life's origins allowed to be taught. It took a very ugly and public trial, along with the rants of H.L. Mencken (the infamous anti-Christian journalist who covered the trial), for Darwin's theory of evolution to enter the classroom.

Speaking of trials, for centuries every witness in court has been required to place his hand on the Bible and swear before God that he would tell the whole truth and nothing but the truth. Why the Bible? Why not the Koran or some other religious text? The answer is simple: America was founded as a Christian nation.

Americans in the nineteenth and early twentieth century allowed newcomers to join in their liberty celebration, with the lone provision that they abide by the laws of the land and respect our traditions—both of which came from Biblical teachings.

Today, a cursory look at Western society reveals that lack of consistency and respect for our Judeo Christian heritage and tradition has left much of the civilized world in ethical shambles. Ask any one of the millions of Muslims that live in our predominantly Christian society why they live here and they will probably point to our Constitution and our courts. These modern immigrants craved the same freedoms that early visitors to Staten Island did. Make no mistake: our First Amendment protects both our and their religious expressions, just as our judicial system protects both us and them from religious extremism.

THOSE PIOUS LIBERTARIANS

As much as proponents of liberalism might deny it, even the Puritan colonists held a high regard for freedom along with a strong and sometimes heavy-handed application of morality in jurisprudence. Ironically, even though they were strongly religious, their view of the world outside of themselves was much like progressive modernists today. Using the same kind of reasoning that liberals do to support abortion and selective discrimination, the Puritans supported slavery and selective separatism.

Even with their obvious flaws, the reason that Puritans are significant when discussing moral clarity in America is that it was they who developed a "civil Body Politick . . . for the General good of the Colony. . . ." Historically known as the Mayflower Compact, this agreement was the first political document to be written in the New World. Think about it: religious separatists were first in the history of modern humanity to develop what we would loosely consider a democratic-republic, where just and fair laws were established to protect individual rights.

It was also the Puritans who helped shape religion, social life, and government in North America in conjunction with the moral code of God. Their strong belief in education led them to establish both Harvard and Yale and to require a system of grammar schools in the colonies.

It is worth noting that even before the New England colonies were getting started, the colony of Jamestown had been eking out an existence in eastern Virginia. Jamestown was the first in

North America to establish a parliamentary style of government with its own bi-cameral House of Burgesses.

Without a doubt, Jamestown was the most "English" of all the early colonies as most of its citizens were Anglicans and not as bent on establishing religious freedom as their northern counterparts were. Yet, it was here, over a hundred years after Jamestown's founding, that Washington, Jefferson, Hamilton, and other Virginia farmers met to decide the fate of Virginia and the rest of the colonies regarding their relationship to King George III.

Rule by the people and for the people (albeit wealthy white landowners) was the *modus operandi* as a majority of these men were fed up with illegal and unjust taxation by the Democrats—uh, I mean the king.

The Jamestown meeting was significant because while the various religious groups were radically different in matters of dogma, they were united in following the same standards of morality as their fathers had. Egalitarianism or not, Puritans, Deists, Unitarians, and Anglicans all understood that matters of behavior radically affected, at the least, life here on earth.

"THOU SHALT NOT KILL" . . . BUT WHY?

Throughout our nation's history, Americans have continually kept traditional Judeo Christian ethics as the standard by which we set our moral compass. It is hard to get beyond the fact that Christianity has played the major, if not the *only*, role in guarding the morality of our nation . . . so remind me again why can't we display or promote these traditions on public property?

I'm always amused by those strict "separation of church and state" groups, Americans for the Separation of Church and State, People for the American Way, the American Atheists, and others that claim law does not or should not reflect personal religious beliefs. After all, aren't religious beliefs the most personal of all beliefs? How can law *not* reflect personal beliefs, religious or otherwise? Is not law the place we encapsulate our corporate views of civility and community and their relationship to the universe?

For example, it is illegal to murder (at least that's what we say officially). Christian Americans (and even many non-Christians) recognize that the law against murder is a direct result of Western acknowledgement of the Sixth Commandment—Thou Shalt Do No Murder.

Those who claim that this is simply a good law without religious context because it prevents one person from taking the life of another must explain why others must keep this law. "Loving your neighbor" does not necessarily come naturally, you know. And how do they explain laws against assisted suicide? Or euthanasia? Or infanticide? Or do they?

How can any laws be valid without a moral code to back them up?

Consider some countries whose laws are not based on Christian principles. For many centuries in the Philippines and other Southeast Asian countries, headhunting was legal and encouraged as part of religious practice, even as recently as the twentieth century. In the Middle East, it is still legal for a family to stone to death a relative if that person has had sexual relations before marriage. Some Asian religious sects allow for children of divorce to be drowned. Prior to the advent of Christianity in Scotland, aged and ailing Gaelic kings were routinely killed by other clan members as part of their customs and traditions. The list goes on and on.

Judeo Christian tradition positively shaped the founding of the United States, its judicial system, and its formation of moral norms, preventing tyranny in our governing bodies with appropriate checks and balances. Because of the preservation of this tradition, people like Maureen Dowd are given the liberty to write scathing anti-conservative rants without fear of being imprisoned. The reverence for Christian morality, as passed down by our forefathers, has given liberty its legs to stand on, allowing conservative commentators like me the opportunity to proclaim loudly the downfalls of progressive modernism without concern for my personal well-being. Even the Dixie Chicks and Ted Turner can be as obnoxious as they want without fear of repercussions from the government and the general public (except perhaps in record sales). Our nation's "dangerous" Christian morality protects both its adherents and its outspoken critics from physical harm.

The challenge Middle America faces as we strengthen our forces in the cultural war is to turn the tide of the destruction and decay left over from a culture that has embraced a materialistic worldview throughout the twentieth century. Ours is a nation that thought it could live outside Judeo Christian morality, and we are paying for it. Not just in our personal lives, but in immoral corruptions in our legal, political, and corporate systems.

If materialism is correct, if nothing abstract can be ascertained, then *morality* is a meaningless word. Without objective standards, our biological makeup and surrounding environment dictate our values, and the only cultural creed is that no one can tell you what to do or impose their values on you. Anyone searching for social parameters—the code of ethics we once took for granted—is hard-pressed to find any boundaries in the public square. What remains is a variety of *suggestions*—all of them right and none of them right, depending on who you ask. As we endure the tyrannical whims of absolute moral relativism, subjectivism rules the day. Putting all jokes aside, President Clinton's explanation of what *is* means is the perfect example of this line of thinking. Even language can be reinvented when subjectivism is king.

Moral relativists want us to believe that there is nothing to fight about, no right or wrong to concern us. Then they abandon their relative stance to wage war over "social injustice" and "intolerance." How can they use phrases like "class warfare" and "No Justice, No Peace" if everything is relevant and there is no foundation upon which to base justice?

Truth and justice exist, but not in the flimsy ideals promoted on the televisions and radios of Middle America for the last half century. Truth and justice do not change with cultural winds. They are bedrock realities, instilled in humanity by the hand of a Divine Creator.

THE IMPOSSIBILITY OF TEACHING NOTHING

Senator Rick Santorum had this to say regarding the left's insistence on removing faith from the public forum:

Given the stereotypes about religion that prevail in America today, one might have expected that a state throbbing with so much religious enthusiasm would rapidly become a haven for bigotry and radical fundamentalism—a kind of 17th century Tehran.

He is right. Liberals have even compared the views of the religious right to Nazis. They insist that until every fragment of religion is removed from public society, America will not reach its intolerant, liberated ideal. Do they realize that it is impossible to teach nothing? If America removes its Judeo Christian values, others will replace them (and indeed already have). The idea of a civil religion or a national morality free of any sectarian influence is a myth. All forms of morality, even moral relativism, are based on presuppositions about the world which cannot be empirically proved.

In other words, the behavior codes that we follow are built upon a foundation of "faith" in our understanding of the universe and human nature. Even the unbeliever is ultimately bound by his "faith" that God does not exist, that there is no heaven or hell, and, therefore, no judgment following death. As much stock as atheists put in the scientific community to prove that the realm of the supernatural does not exist, they must still have faith that no future developments will disprove their theories, and that science has not miscalculated in reaching its conclusion.

Once people are converted to atheism, all decisions about how to govern men's lives are then based upon the notion that human nature is a product of some cosmic accident. Man becomes the center of the universe, making himself the god who has the capacity to fix all societal ills. Through constant research—the unquenchable and never-ending search for life's answers—men and women following this kind of mindset are easily susceptible to utopian ideals and vain fantasies. Like dieting fads, societal "saviors" (usually in the form of one *ism* or another) come and go. Yesterday's yoga is today's Kabbalah.

The revolving door of religions is relatively new for our society. America has traditionally respected its Judeo Christian heritage. For centuries, U.S. citizens elected leaders who understood that America was founded upon principles that rewarded virtue and character, hard work and responsibility. (The terms *virtue* and *character* had specific definitions, too. Not ones easily manipulated to jibe with the reigning social theory.) For example, two highly esteemed virtues in early America were chastity and fidelity. Both were expected of citizens, for they ensured that strong families, the most fundamental of all "governing" bodies in society, would be established, and the future generations of Americans would be secured.

Those virtues have vanished from modern American consciousness. No public school Web site advocates anything close to chastity and fidelity. Instead, they have been replaced with "values" unfamiliar to the nineteenth-century ear—*tolerance, diversity, safety*—none of which actually instill character in children. Instead, they indoctrinate kids into the world of political correctness and the agenda of progressive liberalism.

So how does a society frame its beliefs on chastity and fidelity? Are these morals as "self-evident" as the truths Jefferson spoke of in the Declaration? Certainly not to our base natures, especially not to that of males. Given men's physical makeup, many would not choose chastity or monogamy if there were no repercussions for not doing so. Something or someone must challenge them to transcend that base nature and become the protectors and providers of their families. Humanity needs an objective truth to give our lives meaning and dignity.

Ultimate truth finds its authority in an object or being that transcends our physical world. If humans are truly honest with ourselves, we admit that we are composed in such a self-centered, incomplete way that we could never, either individually or corporately, create a society that is successful without the help of a transcendent object or being. Otherwise, if we really are in charge of defining truth, which one or group of us gets to define it? Whose definition of right and wrong is correct?

Contrary to the beliefs of those who exalt the precepts of the Enlightenment (one being that man has the potential to perfect himself), we must understand that man's rationale is not merely incomplete; it is impoverished. Look around at our communities overrun by delinquency and dereliction. Our inner cities as well as our country clubs are filled with broken lives, homes, and spirits. It seems that for all the promises of enlightened reason, our society is in dire need of consistent moral landmarks.

WHAT IS TRUTH?

No matter how many times a society reinvents itself with new versions of "correctness," it always comes back to some basic fundamentals. Amazingly, regardless of a people's national, racial, ethnic, or religious backgrounds, these fundamentals are the same. For example, coveting, slander, and murder are "sins" in a moral code that is common to all religions and belief systems throughout the world. C.S. Lewis wrote in his excellent book, *The Abolition of Man*, that there are basic "first principles" common to every civilization. To deny this fact is to reject Reason and to delve into the irrational. Lewis writes that holding to these principles:

> Is the Way in which the universe goes on, the Way in which things everlastingly emerge, stilly and tranquilly, into space and time. It is also the Way in which every man should tread in imitation of that cosmic and supernatural progression, conforming all activities to that great exemplar.

Identifying this common thread between different sects and religions as the *Tao*, Lewis goes on to explain that the Tao " . . . is the doctrine of objective value, the belief that certain attitudes are really true, and others are really false. . . ." In other words, anything outside of this doctrine of objective truth, the Tao, has no foundation in reality. Those who follow Judeo Christian teaching would refer to it as wisdom, often described in the Book of Proverbs, Chapters 1–3:

> Wisdom calls aloud outside; She raises her voice in the open squares . . . Happy is the man who finds wisdom, And the man who gains understanding; For her proceeds are better than the profits of silver, And her gain

than fine gold. She is more precious than rubies, And all the things you may desire cannot compare with her. Length of days is in her right hand, Her ways are ways of pleasantness, And all her paths are peace. She is a tree of life to those who take hold of her. And happy are all who retain her.

To find wisdom requires objectivity. It is a "something" (*the* Something) that can be sought, whose finding and application brings our daily lives the true freedom we so desperately want.

It seems the definitions of *freedom* and *liberty* are elusive in today's society. *Webster's Dictionary* defines *freedom* as being the "absence of necessity, coercion, or constraint in choice or action." For a segment of American society, that meaning fits nicely into their personal agendas. But one only has to carry the idea to its furthest potential to realize that freedom in this sense is not only dangerous, but also fatal to individual and community alike.

In the extreme liberal understanding of freedom, I should be allowed to sell junk bonds on the Internet to any unsuspecting fool and not be charged with a crime. Heroin and crack cocaine dealers should be considered heroes instead of villains for bringing jobs and income into lower-class neighborhoods. Murderers should be praised for their "bravery" in overcoming their puny Judeo-Christian conscience by taking the life of someone who was getting in the way of their pursuit of happiness. This is freedom, ala Nietzsche.

To sort out the confusion on what *freedom* truly means,

let's review some basics. To begin with, the very idea that we should be free requires "belief" itself—it is not simply the result of instinct. Accordingly, our belief in freedom must stem from a source: a moral system telling us that freedom is good and right. (There's that *moral* word again. Try as we may, we can't escape it.)

But if freedom is an extension of morality, where does morality come from? Is it from a higher authority, something or someone extraneous to our world, or does mankind get to make up the laws of humanity as we go along? Is it primitive to believe that there must be a final authority on what is good and evil, an authority who judges the difference?

THE PERILS OF FREEDOM

Decades after the "free love" revolution left its mark (and its illegitimate children and sexual epidemics) on our culture, millions of Americans are still duped into believing that Judeo-Christian morality and ethics is the real enemy to freedom when reality is the opposite. Today's *freedom* equals "license" (notice that "license" and "licentious" have the same root word), often leading to difficulties, disease, and even death. Instead of fulfillment, it brings bondage. I am sure many of the millions of Americans behind bars reveled in their "freedom" from society's rules—until they were caught. Their distortion of freedom led to captivity. Middle America needs to pray that our society's residual biblical values will limit this kind of "freedom's" progress.

Don't we all end up appreciating being warned by someone

in authority that the road we are taking leads to trouble? Does a mother show love by allowing her toddler the freedom to play in the street? Or by giving her teenager the liberty to stay out all night? Don't children come to despise parents who do not care enough or are too afraid to instruct them in the rules of life?

Biblical precepts actually enhance liberty in the way the founding fathers intended. In fact, liberty is impossible to achieve and maintain without faithfully adhering to them. As my bishop has said on numerous occasions, God didn't give us the Ten Commandments to take away our fun—He provided them for our own health and safety.

Most progressive liberals will qualify their definition of freedom with statements like "as long as it doesn't hurt anyone else" or "as long as you don't offend anyone." The problem with that is the misuse of freedom has already hurt and offended the majority of the citizens of Middle America.

SPEAK NO EVIL, HEAR NO EVIL, FIGHT NO EVIL

When carried out to its full extent, secularism can affect the life of the simplest churchgoer among us. We have all heard the stories, perhaps lived them . . . a town, sued over its "offensive" nativity scene; an employee, forced to remove the religious calendar from his cubicle; a child, punished for bringing a Bible to Show and Tell.

And what has been Middle America's response?

We assuage our "outrage" by yelling at the television or calling a friend to rant for a while. Or maybe we'll fire off a few distraught emails to Oprah.

Rarely do we make radical changes in our own daily lives. Rarely do we discuss our values with those outside of our safety cushion. Rarely do we make a difference.

When we feel threatened by the rapid advance of liberalism, it is easier to blame government agencies, the media, public education, and the homosexual and abortion-rights activists themselves for the cultural corruption around us. But even if they are guilty of hijacking our culture's values, we still must ask, "Who allowed them so much latitude? Who stepped back from the frontline of battle and permitted them to occupy the land?"

Liberal tyranny reigns only because we are either too lazy or too afraid to stand on the watchtower and warn the people of the coming hordes of barbarians. For example, a 2005 poll showed that 87 percent of Christians favor the Bible over Darwin in the explanation of the origins of human life. But how many of those polled even knew that the teaching of evolution replaced the teaching of creation more than thirty years ago? The battle to have creationism taught in our public schools alongside evolution is one that most Christians don't know or don't care is being lost.

It appears that the Christian community is desperately trying to win the approval of a secular world that only wants to marginalize them. It reminds me of that line in *Braveheart* where William Wallace chastises the Scottish nobility for their constant willingness to bow down to their cruel English masters: "You're so concerned with squabbling for the scraps from

Longshank's table that you've missed your God-given right to something better."

Have America's Christians sold their birthright for a bowl of lentil soup? It seems that the body of Christ is more than willing to assist in its marginalization with the hopes that the cultural elite will give them a courtesy pat on the back. Not only do we cower down to secularist charges of "intolerance" and "judging," not only do we abandon unpopular convictions in an effort to please, we also join in the moral decline. The way we spend our money, our time, and our energies reveals if our treasure is truly in heaven, or if it is here on earth with those who don't believe in heaven. As liberalism grows in dominance over every institution in our society, Christians will indeed receive a pat on the back—right out the door of cultural relevance.

Liberals have also gotten away with elevating relativism because too many Christians think that the glue that holds this great country together is about everyone just making "good choices." In the same way that a person might look at the war in Iraq and say, "Why can't we all just get along?" these naïve Christians have bought the lie that all ideas have acceptable merit and it is wrong to judge another person's opinion or stand for absolutes. Their shallow logic puts grave moral decisions on the level of choosing what soda to buy. After all, some people like Diet Coke, and some like Sprite, but at least each person is having a drink, and let's not look down on a person just because she prefers less calories and no caffeine.

This lukewarm morality exists in church teachings throughout the United States as many church leaders suffer from the embarrassment of believing in absolute truth. Christian timidity runs throughout our society as Christian politicians, celebrities, judges, pastors, and priests overly apologize for the teachings of the church that have been handed down to us for over two thousand years.

Why don't we rise up in force against the diabolical plot of progressive liberalism? Why allow them to eradicate our religious expression and elevate unbridled sexual expression and other ungodly causes? Shouldn't the religious community influence the culture and not the other way around?

No, despite the sneers and snubs of the more "enlightened" ones around us, the church today is not irrelevant. If we are so irrelevant to today's progressive thinkers, why do thousands of homosexuals demand approval from the same church whose teachings have prohibited sodomy for the last two thousand years (or longer if you're counting the Torah)? If the church's moral authority is of no effect, and has no affect on them, then why do they care what Pope John Paul the Great had to say *ex cathedra* about issues of sexuality and abortion? Why shiver with rage at the words of Jim Dobson, Jerry Falwell, Richard Land, or Lou Sheldon?

If the church were truly irrelevant, Billy Graham and thousands of other American clergy would be moonlighting as insurance salesmen due to empty pews. There would be no Christian music industry. There would be no powerful ministries reaching the poor. The church is not irrelevant because Jesus is not irrelevant. We have the numbers, the obligation, and the God-given moral authority to push back the darkness in our society. *So if you are as conservative and religious as you say you are, is your sword sharpened for battle?*

THE MARKETING OF THE MODERN CHURCH

In modern times, God's people have been increasingly ostracized in the public square, with Evangelicals being stigmatized as the last group on earth you would belong to if you really are a caring individual. The animosity is not limited toward a few obnoxious rightwing commentators. Look at the many anti-Christian Web sites out there and you'll read all kinds of "proof" about how Christianity has been the one reason for the downfall of Western civilization.

Perhaps in response, the church in America has tried to show its modern, softer side. Desperate for new ways to get its message across, pop Christianity has embraced every passing fad from the seeker-friendly church growth philosophy to the name-it-and-claim-it word of faith movement. It is said that the church always reflects the culture. Today's churches look more like businesses with well-staffed marketing departments than places of worship where a person can come to confess his sins, receive prayer, hear the Gospel preached, and partake in Holy Communion. When the pastor of a church takes his strategies from a CEO on the Fortune 500, be prepared to witness a few compromises in true worship and ministry for the sake of presentation.

Consider the music and publications that come from much of our Christian culture today, especially that of the American Evangelical. For every style of pop music offered on the local station, there is a Christianized version of the same—rap, punk, bubblegum pop, you name it. Church music sounds like a version of America's Top 40, only cheaper. In the same way, Christian education oftentimes resembles a baptized version of liberal pedagogical methods even though more classical forms have so much more to offer. And while some evangelicals complain about the complicated liturgy of the Orthodox Church, try getting past the bureaucracy of ministers, associate ministers, and recreational ministers to talk to the pastor of a megachurch (that is if you can navigate your way through the gymnasium).

HOLY ROLLING DOWN THE SLIPPERY SLOPE

Through the years, the Progressive Movement gained influence over every institution, including religious ones. In June of 2004, the Episcopal Church of the United States of America (ECUSA) elected its first openly and active gay bishop. Many in the denomination declared it a victory for unity and diversity, while others saw it more apocalyptically, believing the end of the church had begun since church leaders were advocating a lifestyle that contradicts the teachings of the Bible. Either way, the election of Bishop Gene Robinson was, perhaps, the culmination of something that had been developing in religious denominations for decades. In the name of being "progressive," religious leaders began to challenge core Christian tenets and make up new rules of biblical interpretations.

As far back as the 1970s, many denominations began to compromise the boundaries of sexuality along with fundamental church doctrines. One of the most notorious promoters of a radically new version of the gospel is Bishop John Shelby Spong of New Jersey, a bishop in the Episcopal Church. Included in his pantheon of ill-conceived notions of Christianity are his rejection of Jesus' virgin birth and resurrection. Spong also encourages belief in the non-canonical Gnostic writing, the Gospel of Thomas, which gives a vastly different account of Christ's relationship to Mary Magdalene.

I remember debating Bishop Spong in the mid-nineties. We were panelists on a leading television talk show to discuss social policy. I didn't know who Spong was theologically, yet assumed it would be a civil discussion regarding poverty. Boy was I wrong! As somewhat of a Christian novice, I assumed the bishop would know more than I did about the essence of Christian doctrine. Instead, I found myself reciting to him the words of the Apostles Creed! If there ever was a time that I appreciated a simple faith in mere Christianity, it was then.

Although many in the ECUSA still hold to traditional doctrine and practice, Spong mustered several faithful comrades-in-arms before his departure. His crusade to destroy absolute faith in confused or hurting seekers continues. He and many like him, including the Reverend Barry Lynn of Americans United to Separate Church and State, have been using cunning tactics to spew their new brand of Christianity that espouses abortion, homosexuality, and animal rights (the new term is *speciesism*).

In one diocese in Pennsylvania, Bishop Charles threatened to close down several churches that would not allow a lesbian bishop to preach in their pulpits. On other occasions, he has deposed priests who remain faithful to the traditional teachings of the church. Throughout the entire institution, the ECUSA is fraught with similar predicaments. It makes you wonder what President George Washington would say if he could see what has happened to the church he attended today!

Other denominations have either walked in lock-step with the ECUSA down the road of moral decadence, or are following their lead. Among them is the United Church of Christ, considered by many to be the "cutting edge" of radical liberation theology—it was the first denomination to ordain an openly gay man, in 1972. Other groups include the Evangelical Lutheran Church of America (ECLA) and the United Methodist Church (UMC), both of which have experimented with church doctrine that pertains to human sexuality.

The ECUSA is a good illustration of the broader moral cultural war being waged in our nation today. The sad thing is that the church should be the guardian of truth, not the promoter of avant-garde experimentalism. The church and its leaders have a responsibility for how they lead society. Scripture has some specific words of warning for teachers:

> Not many of you should presume to be teachers, my brothers, because you know that we who teach will be judged more strictly. *James 3:1*

Jesus said in Matthew that those who lead the naïve and suffering astray have something to fear:

> Whoever causes one of these little ones who believe in Me to sin, it would be better for him if a millstone were hung around his neck, and he were drowned in the depth of the sea.

Paul warned in 2 Timothy about an immoral time that sounds much like today:

> For the time will come when men will not put up with sound doctrine. Instead, to suit their own desires, they will gather around them a great number of teachers to say what their itching ears want to hear.

Running from our identity as Christians in an attempt to make ourselves appear "normal" or "relevant" to society only destroys any credibility we still have left with the secular world. Furthermore, it robs us of our own birthright to be the sons and daughters of the living God. St. Paul defied the Roman officials and Jewish Pharisees, even in the face of death, for he understood all too well that to lay hold of Christ was to lay hold of his God-given destiny, his birthright so to speak, the very thing for which he was born and called to be.

A funny cartoon I ran across shows the struggle of today's church to hold onto its beliefs in the middle of an immoral culture. In the cartoon stands a man in a tuxedo, a dog in a wedding dress, and a woman priest performing their marriage. In the back of the church, two traditionalist priests sit with a look of disgust on their faces. One priest leans over to the other and says, "Just one more thing and I'm leaving the church!"

"Just one more thing" . . . if the church turns up its volume on tolerance any higher the way liberals suggest, we will all be deaf.

SOME ISSUES ARE
BLACK AND WHITE

If intensity measures religiosity, then African Americans are the most religious of all Americans. A survey done by the Pew Center a number of years ago showed blacks responded at higher rates than whites that religion plays a "very important" role in their lives. Yet churchgoing blacks continue to overwhelmingly support welfare-state politics and politicians.

Christians of every shade recognize the struggle to live out their faith in their daily lives. Worshipping the Lord is easier than serving Him. Many of Middle America's religious act far different at work on Monday or at a party on Friday than they do at church on Sunday. In the same way, African Americans mistakenly and destructively disconnect the way we express our religious convictions on Sunday and what we do in the voting booth on Tuesday. In church we express convictions that our lives reflect our faith, our choices, and our responsibilities. Yet, we then turn around and buy into a political message that government is the place to turn to solve our problems.

Not long after the first images of post-Katrina appeared, the liberal media pushed charges of racism to the front pages. I was asked to share my thoughts about the situation on television. On my walk to the set, I asked the twenty-year-old white woman escorting me if she was a racist. She turned a little pink and in pure innocence softly said no. Then I asked if it bothered her that a high number of blacks believed that racism was the primary factor in the government response failure. Timidly, she said yes. What makes blacks so shortsighted on concepts of destiny or purpose that the moment a tragedy strikes or any inconvenience or difficulty arises we are so willing to believe that racism is at work rather than God?

Trust issues are not discriminatory. The dollar bill we all carry says, "In God We Trust." But regardless of our race or position in life, as supposed believers in God, do we really trust in Him as the provider of our needs and the protector of our country and family? Secularism has told us to no longer trust in God, but to look to ourselves, the power of the government, and the wisdom of science to answer all the questions of life and to provide for our needs.

Each group buys a part of the lie. Middle-class Christians are tempted to adopt the American value of "self-reliance" and take pride in pulling ourselves up with our own bootstraps. Inner-city African Americans face the temptation to rely not on God or on themselves, but on our government to take care of them. Too often we Christians put our God on the shelf until we are in really dire straits, or only give lip service to Him. We put our faith in government and financial security instead of the God who heals the deepest issues of our souls.

Blacks and whites may both have trust issues, but they haven't been discussing them together. The Christian church in the United States has traditionally been divided along the lines of race with little real opportunity for blacks and whites to join together as one voice.

This unfortunate situation took a positive turn in the election of 2004, when the moral demise of our country was on full display in the movement for homosexual marriage. Even the insidious sin of abortion has not united evangelicals the way homosexual activism has. Both black and white church leaders are now building new alliances to find ways to unite Christians to stand for the restoration of Judeo Christian ethics in the judiciary and political process.

In the black community the homosexual marriage issue proved to mark the beginning of a sea change in black voting behavior. Pastors who voted Democratic all their lives were led out of the Democratic Party by this one issue.

One reason black leaders are so worked up over the homosexual marriage issue is because it fundamentally touches the core concerns they have for their communities. They know that the bedrock on which human lives and communities are constructed is made of spiritual and moral fiber. And they know that the profound social problems in their community—one with the nation's highest rates of new AIDS cases, out-of-wedlock births, and abortions—stem from the shattered state of that bedrock.

These pastors are beginning to grasp that the welfare state and the politics of the liberal left have damaged character in the black community. They know that their community's first order of business is reconstituting its spiritual and moral base. For them, the idea of our society formally abandoning traditional standards of sexual behavior and traditional concepts of marriage and family is outrageous. Black pastors see every day that communities without values and standards do not nurture free people but foster slaves. The last thing that the black community needs is formal institutionalization of our nation's moral decay.

As black and white American Christians unite to defend our

nation's heritage of biblical morality, we want to remember our
true cause and enemy. In the midst of all the rhetoric, spin, and
demonization of the "religious right," the fact is lost that
Christians in fact agree that Americans should have the free will
to believe what they want. We are not crusading against religious
diversity. We just believe that our country should also have an
agreed-upon moral code, and that from the founding of our
nation, that code has been based on Judeo Christian principles.

And who is the enemy of our cause? Think about who is
pressuring today's Christians to keep our faith under wraps. It is
not the people who serve other gods who are demanding our
silence. We are not debating Hindus, Buddhists, or Muslims.
The people so determined to quash our most sacred beliefs are
the progressive liberals we work for, buy from, and watch on TV
everyday.

WHERE DOES THE CHURCH
GO FROM HERE?

"Values Voters" of 2004 owe thanks to another group besides
homosexual activists for focusing us on morality. Though it
may not have registered with our overwhelmingly Protestant
mindsets, the Catholic Church, most notably His Holiness the
late John Paul II, engaged in some of the more obvious moral
battles against the American psyche.

Without the staunch, yet gentle, pastoral and visionary leadership of the pope, especially during the 1990s, it is difficult to
imagine how many more inroads abortion and homosexuality
might have gained in our society. Thanks to His Holiness and

others who speak out to stop our country from killing millions of its own, (and to the mounting chagrin of pro-abortion groups), the number of those who support abortion-on-demand has dwindled tremendously over the last decade. John Paull II's successor, Pope Benedict XVI, makes no bones about his orthodox and traditional approach to Catholic doctrine—abortion and homosexuality are unacceptable and untenable.

Many Protestant denominations and Evangelical groups also continue to hold firm to tradition and practice orthodoxy when it comes to issues of morality. The Southern Baptist Convention (SBC) continues its firm stand against abortion and sexual experimentation. Under the guidance of such leaders as Billy Graham and Richard Land, the SBC has played a major role in holding back the tide of moral relativism. Another new stalwart denomination that stands resilient in its affirmation of traditional Christianity is the Charismatic Episcopal Church (CEC). Headed by Abp. Randolph Adler, the CEC is aggressively becoming a force in movements for life and against the legalization of homosexual marriage. The conservative elements of the Lutheran, Presbyterian, Methodist and other mainline churches have firmed up their convictions, and many independent evangelical mega-churches have engaged in the battle against liberalism front-and-center.

Now I know that it is more comfortable for some Christians to point their fingers at numerous arenas or battlefronts and decide that activism is not necessary to reverse the moral decline in our country. Some will cheer on a few victories and then return to their nice homes to sit on their laurels. Others will look at how the enemy attacked the family life of a few of our heroes like Alan Keyes and Randy Terry and conclude that the costs are too high.

But the costs not to engage in the war are even higher. Need I remind you of other periods in our history when we thought our political and economic apparatus could work independently of religious and moral truths? Liberals in America have positioned their insidious secular humanism into every aspect of our society over the entire last century, and are now today's "experts." Christianity is on the defense, marginalized out of the public square. We had better prepare for a long struggle if we really want to win America's cultural war; the radical far-left agenda did not just manifest itself overnight.

The stakes could not be higher.

Now I know some are asking, "Where's your faith, Star? We know the end of the story, so let's just pray!" Okay then, I will "just pray" as you go back to work tomorrow to implement your company's new domestic partnership benefits for homosexuals. Let's all "just pray" as your fourteen-year-old niece has a Norplant implanted into her arm by her public school nurse without your brother's knowledge or permission. Or let's all "just pray" when your son's first-grade teacher is fired for leading her class in the Pledge of Allegiance. Sorry, but I feel compelled to do more than "just pray" in these corrupt times. Prayer is indeed powerful. And so is action.

Signs everywhere demand that America's believers reassess some of our foundational suppositions. How much longer can we retreat into the walls of our churches, our homes, and our home schools and ignore the battle between good and evil being fought daily in our national culture? How can we continue to work for or buy from companies that publicly advocate and support everything we are morally against? What of our elected representatives and judiciary that have no definitive ethical guidelines? If America's moral foundations are destroyed, what will those dedicated to "living quiet lives in quiet places" for God do?

THE BOTTOM LINE: WHERE ARE WE NOW?

A recent Web search I did gave a sad commentary on America's current priorities.

Just for fun, I decided to go to the Gallup poll Web site to make some comparisons between a couple of polls on moral and social issues. I first checked up on smoking, since for the last fifteen years more and more doctors and lobbyists are speaking out on its dangers. The debate over smoking in public places has heated up so much that the momentum to see a complete ban on smoking in restaurants is supported by 54 percent of the population, and support to have smoking banned *completely* has grown from 10 percent in 1987 to 34 percent in 2005.

After digesting those numbers, I hunted for the public opinion on the topic of abortion. Here is what I found: since 1989, the percentage of people who want *Roe v. Wade* to be left untouched by the Supreme Court has climbed from 58 percent to 68 percent.

Where is the focus the American people, at least according to the polls? Apparently it is not on the nearly one million children killed every year, mostly for "convenience." No, it appears that we are a nation more concerned about the possibility of inhaling a bit of secondhand smoke than saving a helpless fetus.

American society is no longer concerned about the eternal, spiritual, or even psychological consequences of its actions.

It is almost amusing that the same people who scream for the freedom to transmit filth over the airwaves are the same ones who go to court to fight public displays of the Ten Commandments. While fighting for hate-crimes legislation to be used against preachers who publicly denounce sodomy, they argue that moms of twelve-year-olds should "just turn the radio off." It makes one wonder if the sacred and the secular can share the same country anymore.

So when we boil it all down, do liberals and conservatives have anything in common besides sharing a country?

Regardless of our religious (or nonreligious) backgrounds, we have to admit that there is one objective morality by which we all abide. In fact, as I mentioned before, every major religion shares a common basic moral code. Isn't that interesting? Whether one is Muslim, Hindu, Buddhist, or Christian, he or she knows that stealing is wrong. Fidelity in marriage and the sin of adultery are universally recognized, regardless of sociological differences. The husband who lives in Great Britain and is married to one woman (as prescribed by law) will become very angry and/or greatly depressed if another man has an affair with his wife. You will find the same sentiments from the African tribal chief. Although he may have seven wives, they are still his wives and do not belong to any other man. These common inner values—dare we say "absolute truths"—had to come from somewhere. Christians believe Someone put them inside of us.

In addition to agreeing on at least some standards of propriety (all Americans, for example, know to be quiet in an elevator, to use our turn signal, to say "bless you" after sneezes, and to never grab a borderline fair ball during the World Series at a Major League baseball park), we also share a few other things in common: For one, Americans generally desire to be a moral people, or at least a people that looks to be moral. If not, there would be no such things as confessionals. There must certainly be a connection between the number of active churches in the United States and the desire for morality. (I'm certain many liberals will object to that statement by saying that the Church has conditioned us through guilt to want to confess our sins or that *sin* is a social construct no longer needed in today's modern age of enlightenment.)

Our nation, Western civilization, indeed the entire world, has been or is currently obsessed with some kind of code of behavior. What that code is or should be is the sticking point, but it is evident that almost every one of us suffers from a condition known as conscience. As polarized as we are, we forget that sometimes. Why else would an organization name itself People for the Ethical Treatment of Animals (PETA) unless they believed that animals deserved some form of respect from humans and that there really is a set of ethics (however subjective and malleable that may be) to which we must all ascribe in our treatment of those animals? Why did Cindy Sheehan stage a protest against President Bush and the War in Iraq unless she felt something was morally repugnant with our foreign policy?

Senator John Kerry, whose voting record on abortion has been astoundingly deplorable, once stated that "Values are not just words, values are what we live by. They're about the causes that we champion and the people we fight for." What causes John Kerry was championing is still left to vain imaginations, but he admits there must be some beliefs worth fighting for. Even the ultra-feminist Gloria Steinem acknowledged that values must be present when she said, "We can tell our values by looking at our checkbook stubs." Of course she was being facetious, but what was she fighting for, other than her own brand of morality and justice? In the hullabaloo of all the chatter over diversity and tolerance, we each are fighting for a kind of morality. The question is, whose version of morality is best for our society?

TRUTH: PICK YOUR VERSION!

Middle Americans must decide who will be their guide on the road to truth. Here are some summaries of what is true for two opposite ends of the moral spectrum in our culture today, secularism and Christianity.

SECULARISM'S VIEW OF SEXUALITY:

If it feels good, do it! The liberal answer to premarital sex—condoms and sex education in schools; the answer to an unplanned pregnancy—abortion; the answer to AIDS among heroine addicts—clean needles. Adhering to the secular view that man is without a soul, all solutions remain on the materialistic level.

Since man is considered just another one of many species and is without any inherent worth (unless he is to donate his organs to another human), then he becomes expendable. Today, groups concerned about overpopulation strongly advocate both abortion and sterilization (sometimes forced). As qualifications for membership into the human race (unborn children need not apply) continue to narrow, infanticide and euthanasia become a more "sensible" means for thinning out unnecessary burdens on society.

This secular thinking also explains the reason why groups such as the Man/Boy Love Association have been able to make headway with some liberal professors and psychological associations. If we are only the products of billions of years of evolution, then sexual behavior, no matter how abhorrent it may appear to us, is just another expression of our species. Should there be limits to that expression? Not according to the progressive liberal—the morés of the past must constantly be reexamined and reinterpreted to fit the demands and "discoveries" of an ever-changing, ever-evolving society.

CHRISTIANITY'S VIEW OF SEXUALITY:

The person who holds to Judeo Christian beliefs understands from the beginning that God is the focal point of the universe. Man is created in His image, the *Imago Deo*, and therefore has an inherent worth that goes beyond any usefulness or goodness that he may offer society. Just the mere fact that he exists makes each individual unique, and thus born with unalienable rights from his Creator. This is why abortion is so devastating to the Christian—the abortionist assumes the role of God and forcibly destroys the life of another human who is also created in the *Imago Deo*.

In the Christian worldview, each man and woman is also born with a soul that will one day see eternal judgment or eternal life, the obvious reason why mankind has always had to wrestle with issues of conscience, sin, and guilt. For the Christian, morality is unchangeable, for it comes from God, the unchangeable, irresistible force of eternity.

Issues of sexuality are issues of the soul. Sex is more than a physical act with tangible repercussions: sex is the sharing of one's soul with another. It goes beyond the base element of lust to serve as the concrete expression of a man's ultimate love for his wife, and vice-versa. This is why it is so tragic to hear about school districts cheapening sex by encouraging sexual experimentation among children. This is also the reason why so many Christians are against the distribution of condoms and sex education in public schools.

For the Christian, abstinence is chosen not just to prevent an unwanted pregnancy; it also prevents the spirit from being tragically damaged through an improper union. This is also why homosexuality in general, and homosexual marriage in particular, is strongly resisted in Congress by conservative Representatives and Senators. It pervades an act that God had originally intended for good.

Along with these moral truths, it is extremely important to point out that, regardless of how perfect a moral code may be, Christianity understands that humanity is fallen. Regardless of how good humanity's intentions may be or how hard we try to become perfect, we are in a constant state of sin. Not only is it within our potential to sin, it occurs whether we wish it to or not. As St. Paul stated in Romans, I do what I hate—my spirit is at war with my flesh.

Fortunately, the God of Christianity is one of great benevolence, and redemption is the constant theme throughout Scripture. This is the core message of the Gospel—God in Christ reconciling the world to Himself: not counting men's sins against them. As a result of His great mercy, Christians feel compelled to offer the same mercy to all of humanity.

THE SECULAR ANSWER TO POVERTY:

Because of the oppressive, greedy majority, we have a permanent underclass. This is not fair. In addition to giving them money and support (since there's no way they could have the initiation and inner resources to help themselves), government should take as much as it can from the rich. They have enough anyway. In the meantime, since there is such a large group of impoverished, less educated people, liberals should keep them voting for their policies and candidates by reminding them how those rich, white Republicans don't care about them.

THE CHRISTIAN ANSWER TO POVERTY:

Jesus said that the poor will always be here. He also said if a man wants the "shirt off your back" (Star's paraphrase), give him your coat too. Mercy and grace are the ultimate law of God, and Christianity charges mankind to reflect His mercy both in word and in deed. Through various faith-based organizations and volunteerism, Christian groups offer more charitable donations than any other secular or religious organizations in the United States, or the world for that matter. (Did you notice that Islamic countries do little or nothing to benefit the poor and needy in their own countries, let alone the world?) When we give, we need to also help meet the deeper needs of the poor by helping to heal the poverty of their souls. We also want to encourage them to live responsible lives, so that they can have self-dignity and be mature citizens of our country.

NOTE: *Prior to my conversion to Christianity and conservative politics, I believed the liberal propaganda that everything was centered on class warfare and race, which was another way of saying that the entire universe was centered on me. That meant getting a welfare check twice a month and living a roller coaster reckless life. My mind—and my future—remained closed. It wasn't until God in His infinite mercy allowed me to experience a very dark emptiness that I became vulnerable, able to lay all my excuses and fear down and take an honest look at myself. When we finally surrender our self-will, our self-interests, and our personal political agendas, we find Truth staring us right in the face, convicting us of our pride.*

Liberals should be happy to know that consistent religious practice helps poor people to move out of poverty and off the welfare rolls:

[Church attendance] is associated with substantial differences in the behavior of [black male youths from poverty-stricken inner-city neighborhoods] and thus in their chances to "escape" from inner-city poverty. It affects allocation of time, school-going, work activity, and the frequency of socially deviant activity. . . . It is important to recognize that our analysis has identified an important set of variables that separate successful from unsuccessful young persons in the inner city. There is a significant number of inner-city youth, readily identifiable, who succeed in escaping that pathology of inner-city slum life.

There is not a more profound example of how biblical values enhance liberty than in people who are able to escape poverty and financial crises through living out their faith.

HOW SECULARISM DEALS WITH THE QUESTIONS OF LIFE:

Post-modern society has become frustrated with the fact that the all-supreme god of science has not been able to solve much of anything. Sure, technology has provided us with some cool gadgets to ease the pain of the suffering soul, but it has not found the cure to a grieving heart or even prevented the growth of the drug culture.

Even more so, progressive technology and beliefs have not been able to solve the "guilt factor" in the heart of every individual: it has no ability to absolve mankind of the sin that ails him. And in its frustration, it has only offered "alternative" solutions. Some of these solutions involve man trying to perfect himself through physical training, scholarship, or good works. Other solutions involve addictive substances or illicit behavior, leading a person to violate his God-given conscience in order to fill the void in his soul.

HOW CHRISTIANITY DEALS WITH THE QUESTIONS OF LIFE:

Christians who take their faith seriously believe that every human being, regardless of skin color or political affiliation, is created in the image of God. Every person is valuable and deserves protection from those who seek to take his or her life. Matters of baptism and salvation are matters of life and death. Opposition to homosexuality, abortion, and stem-cell research are not just political issues or matters of personal likes or dislikes. Rather, these are issues that affect the very "air" we breathe since our behavior has both earthly and eternal consequences, either good or bad. For us, to destroy a human life is to destroy a created being whom God loves with great passion.

Truth as prescribed by religious tradition requires that man give up his hold on his faulty belief in the ability of the human mind to overcome all societal ills or to master all questions of life, and place his trust in the Unknown. It is when we come to the recognition that we are nothing without God—that our hope in the human potential to save ourselves is recognized as vain—it is then that we reach the very bottom, that hard, rocky bottom, and find our true identity in the Creator of the Universe. Honesty and wisdom become commodities worth more than all the gold in the world, and we accept the *Tao* not as a choice but as the immutable, eternal reality for all humanity.

Cynics will say that the religiously contented are mere sheep, and many Christians are quite defensive to this charge.

But I fully embrace it, for it is true—we are mere sheep in a world full of mystery. To be contented with the fact that the majority of those mysteries will be left unsolved is not the mark of stupidity, but of humility. It is the arrogant who wish to pry into everything and make premature judgments about wonders such as the origins of the universe and mankind. It is the arrogant who hold to the notion that mankind has the potential to perfect himself. And it is the arrogant who become the most frustrated with their surroundings and loved ones when their Great Society yields nothing but destruction, anger, and death. In the end, it is their cynicism toward religion, especially toward any belief in the scandalous love of God for mankind, that creates a nihilistic world without hope for anything but ashes and dust.

JOINING THE BATTLE

When we peel away the layers of class envy, race, and even the cultural war itself, we are left with one question: "What am I here on earth to do?" Liberals have tried to answer that question for us by categorizing people into groups, then labeling the groups for packaging and redistribution. For the liberal, we are nothing more than different breeds of cattle with only a few ranch hands deciding who remains in the pasture, and who ends up in the slaughterhouse. Nothing is about destiny or purpose.

Far too often, we humans crave that type of "branding" and wear our label as though, more than anything else, it identifies the core essence of who we are. We like that a generalized

identity helps us to know our place in this world and to identify others who are in "our group." *Oh, so you're a white conser-*
vative homemaker from the red states? Me, too! Inhabiting our
label also simplifies matters in terms of introspection and personal judgment. If others tell us who we are and what we believe,
we don't have to deal with life's ambiguities.

Labeling can be useful at times. Throughout this book I
have labeled people as "liberals," "radicals," and "conservatives."
But by using these terms, it is not so much the individuals I am
trying to identify as it is the ideological philosophy and politics
they adopt.

In fact, every one of us has a natural proclivity to resist the
idea of labels because they simply do not get at the heart of who
we actually are: Americans, blacks, whites, conservatives,
Democrats, liberals, Republicans, or even Independents. I'm not
just a "Southerner" or a "Reaganite." I am first and foremost a
Christian. The political labels of "black" and "woman" fall to the
wayside as I embrace Truth and walk in it. I may have voted for
Bush, but my allegiance is to Christ. For most of us, our desig-
nated cultural label doesn't touch upon the fundamental basics
of who we are as human beings trying to make our way through
a very tough life.

Before we can effectively contribute to the heated political
debates raging in our country, we must give very careful con-
sideration to the fundamental questions of life and not fall prey
to whatever is culturally en vogue in any given generation. If
Americans are willing to sift through all of our political views
and come to the very nucleus of who we are, we find that it is
our beliefs about the universe, humanity, and God that shape

our perspectives on life in general and our individual life's purpose in particular.

The cultural war in America is actually a struggle over society reconciling itself to "nature's God." Its outcome determines whether we will find in ourselves, once again, a yearning for authentic freedom, the salve that restores clarity of vision and makes truths self-evident. Only through the lens of genuine freedom can we see that, rather than limiting or stifling our freedom, traditional morality protects us from destroying ourselves.

Freedom without consistent values is not freedom at all, regardless of what the progressive liberal school of thought would have us believe. Millions of Americans have already been seduced into trading their God-given individuality and purpose for a materialistic view of the world that strips them of their hearts and souls. This increasing relativism makes devout Christians wary. When a group of people lives by faith in themselves alone, placing an irrational trust in the omnipotence of science and refusing to admit their own sinful nature, civil society collapses upon itself.

The loss of moral value and perspective has weakened our country, making us less free. We must recognize this and start asking and answering some tough questions. If Middle America is willing to participate with God and follow the mandates of a morality that requires self-restraint in our passions and integrity in our actions, we can secure the future freedom of our nation. Our forefathers would ask no less.

It is time to join the battle.

AFTERWORD

Joseph Lowery, the former president of the Southern Christian Leadership Conference, once said, "When America gets a cold, black America gets pneumonia." Few would argue that inner-city America is in robust health. But the good old ordinary middle-class members of America are sick, too. Ill from the ongoing politicization of our society and the breakdown of the traditional values that have been the glue holding together our families and society for centuries. The symptoms of America's "cold" are obvious—skyrocketing rates of divorce and illegitimacy, declining test scores in a politicized and bureaucratized public-school system, the politicization of a legal system that has trampled on its moral foundations, and a rising disregard for the Bible and its teachings. Sure, the chaos shows up worse in black communities. But the corruption is everywhere.

The moral apathy of general American society has bolstered the hopes of those intent on removing any trace of Judeo Christian values from our nation. While most of us sat passively by watching our favorite television shows and playing on the computer, liberalism seeped into every public arena and removed the boundaries set up to guard our nation's children. No more school prayers, no more pledges of allegiance. Once these symbols of morality were gone, liberals' own version of morality stepped in to take charge.

This was no accident. The warped system of values flourishing in our country today deliberately killed the old one.

The plethora of ridiculous statements and absurd causes circulating around our country reveal an agenda gone wild. Bored with their tirades against Yukons and Hummers, liberals' venom has honed in on vile citizen groups like church ladies and boy scouts. Issues of race, equality, and civil rights have been politicized to such a great degree that every other American is hopping on the entitlement train and adopting a victim mentality.

Secularists have learned that if they repeat lies enough, America will believe it. No wonder that in response to one defeat of homosexual marriage in California, the mayor of San Francisco was confident enough to say, "It's just a matter of time."

As Middle America enjoys the unprecedented prosperity that freedom has made possible, we are losing a sense that every benefit has a cost, and that great freedom demands responsibility. It seems the more we acquire, the more irresponsible we become. The easier our lives become, the more we view our bounty as an entitlement.

You may have noticed that one topic raging in our country was strangely absent from these pages. After all, it is en vogue to debate the merits and problems of our troops in Iraq. Perhaps that discussion will take place in another book.

But for now, I have a warning for a Middle America knee-deep in arguments over the military mayhem—both for those proclaiming the unjust evil of the operation, and for those defending it as a necessary evil in the battle for democracy and human rights:

If we are not careful, while American media and political society focuses on the planes flying over Iraq, we will fail to notice the mounting casualties from another war being fought—the battle for morality in our country. The ever-watching world is aware of this war, aware we are on a precipice. Some anticipate our fall.

The United States of America has been a beacon in the night, the city upon a hill, and we can be that again. The election of 2004 was a win for traditional morality, for what is right and sane. But the war is not over. We cannot rest on our laurels and expect, as liberalism teaches, that the government will take care of everything for us. It is up to us to engage in the cultural war and complete the task at hand. Whether our country continues its legacy of lifting up the dual values of freedom and morality depends on you and me.

If Middle America believes there is honor to protect, we must stand up and fight. If not, then we better get used to life in the ghetto.

Bibliography

Belien, Paul. "First Trio 'Married' in The Netherlands." *Brussels Journal.com*, September 26, 2005. http://www.brusselsjournal. com/node/301.

CNN/USA Today/Gallup Poll on abortion opinions. March 21-23, 2005. http://www.religioustolerance.org/abopoll05.htm.

Jessen, Gianna. "An Abortion Survivor." April 22, 1996. http://members. tripod.com/~joseromia/gtext.html.

Johnston, Wm. Robert. "Abortion Statistics and Other Data." http:// www.johnstonsarchive.net/policy/abortion/.

Kovacs, Joe. "Faith Under Fire: Christmas in America Becomes Battleground." *WorldNetDaily.com*, December 14, 2002. http://www. worldnetdaily.com/news/article.asp?ARTICLE_ID=29995.

LaBarbera, Peter. "When a Homosexual Murders a Christian: Media Ignore Mary Stachowicz." *IllinoisFamily.org*, November 17, 2005. http://www.illinoisfamily.org/informed/contentview.asp?c=30009.

"Lawrence v. Texas." *Wikipedia, the Free Encyclopedia.* http://en.wikipedia. org/wiki/Lawrence_v._Texas.

National Gay and Lesbian Task Force. "Texas Voters Approve Anti-Marriage Constitutional Amendment." Press Release, November 8, 2005. http://www.thetaskforce.org/media/release.cfm?release ID=887.

National Right to Life. "Abortion in the United States: Statistics and Trends." http://www.nrlc.org/abortion/facts/abortionstats.html.

Olasky, Marvin. "Blue-State Philosopher." *World Magazine,* November 27, 2004. http://www.worldmag.com/subscriber/displayarticle. cfm?id=9987

Parker, Kathleen. "Parents Take Another Hit in the Culture Wars." *Orlando Sentinel,* November 6, 2005. http://www.orlandosentinel. com/news/opinion/orlparker0605nov06,0,2092861,print. column?coll=orl-cal.

Paul, M.D., Ron. "Federal Courts and the Imaginary Constitution." *LewRockwell.com,* August 12, 2003. http://www.lewrockwell. com/paul/paul120.html.

"Poll: Most Oppose Gay Weddings." *CBSNews.com,* February 24, 2004. http://www.cbsnews.com/stories/2004/02/24/national/ main601 828.shtml.

Saletan, William. "Ass Backwards: The Media's Silence about Rampant Anal Sex." *Slate.com,* September 20, 2005. http://www.slate.com/id/ 2126643/.

Wetzstein, Cheryl. "Sex Content Soars on Prime-time TV." *The WashingtonTimes.com,* November 10, 2005. http://www.washington times.com/national/20051110-120222-2157r.htm.

Will, George. "The Partial-Birth Sensors." *JewishWorldReview.com,* August 21, 2000. http://www.jewishworldreview.com/cols/ will082100.asp.

Zwillich, Todd. "More Sex Content on Teens' TV Survey Shows Increase in Sexual References on Shows Watched by Teenagers." *WebMD Medical News,* Reviewed by Louise Chang, MD, November 09, 2005. http://www.webmd.com/content/Article/115/ 111497.htm.

CPSIA information can be obtained
at www.ICGtesting.com
Printed in the USA
LVOW03s0221110616

492165LV00004BA/9/P